THE CRUCIFIXION OF MAN, A NARRATIVE POEM

Published © 2017 Trieste Publishing Pty Ltd

ISBN 9780649082841

The crucifixion of man, a narrative poem by George Barlow

Edited by Trieste Publishing Pty Ltd.
Cover © 2017

www.triestepublishing.com

GEORGE BARLOW

THE CRUCIFIXION OF MAN, A NARRATIVE POEM

Trieste

THE CRUCIFIXION OF MAN

A Narrative Poem

BY

GEORGE BARLOW

Author of "The Pageant of Life" and "From Dawn to Sunset"

London

SWAN SONNENSCHEIN & CO.

PATERNOSTER SQUARE

1893

CONTENTS.

b

423

Dedication.

TO MY FRIEND,

ARTHUR HERVEY.

THIS book, now bright with dawn, now dark with doom,
  Now full of midday song, I bring you, friend—
Not all conceived in light, nor yet in gloom,
  But in a sphere where light and darkness blend.

I strive in verse to render forth the song
  Of life, to life's strange message I give heed:
But where my Art is faulty, yours is strong,
  And where I fail, you triumph and succeed.

For you in music render forth the psalm
  Of life, aye all its passion, all its power ;
Music can reproduce June's heavenliest calm
  When no breath stirs the frailest cliff-side flower.

And music too can thunder like the seas :
  The world's emotion music can express ;
The saint's thoughts praying on his bended knees,
  The lover's thrill at beauty's first caress.

Music will lead some stricken soul to seek
  Eternal refuge in a Saviour's arms,
Stablish the doubting and uplift the weak,
  Expounding heaven's imperishable charms :

Music will lead a lover to decide
  That this night's starry fires shall point the way
To the sweet robbery of another's bride,
  The sin that cries for blood at dawn of day.

For music stirs in one the lust to storm
  Heaven's breachless walls and unattempted gates,
But draws another towards the perfect form
  Whose sovereign whiteness in the darkness waits.

At music's trumpet one man climbs the skies
  And gathers strength the untrodden heights to win ;
Another dares to meet the queenly eyes
  Whose light makes sinning pure and virtue sin.

The same sweet strain in one girl's heart will wake
  Desire for heavenly joys that never pall,
Possess another, till her swift steps take
  The rose-hung road that leads her to her fall.

One girl will muse : " Is this the heavenly strain
  That sun-bright angels round their Master sing ? "
Another whisper : " In the moonlit lane
  Again to-night my eyes will greet their king ! "

Through music the one Spirit who sways the whole,
  Creates, pulls down, refashions and destroys,
Speaks—ever music is the world's deep soul
  Uttering its giant sorrows, giant joys.

From the first hour when on our planet-home
  Love spake, in depths of moonlit forest heard
Or by some far-off sea's forgotten foam,
  Its priceless first unfathomable word,

From that first hour hath music reigned supreme,
  For music's soul and passion's soul are one;
And music still will reign while young hearts dream
  And while sweet darkness follows on the sun.

All dim strange thoughts we struggle, and in vain,
  To utter—pangs and joys, and hopes and fears—
In music their impassioned utterance gain;
  All human longings sound in human ears.

The past grows vocal, history speaks once more.
  Above dense war-ranks nods Achilles' plume:
Pale Dido weeps upon the loveless shore:
  Masked murder dogs love's steps through Venice' gloom.

At music's touch man's visions all grow real;
  We see the matchless face that Bothwell saw:—
We enter too the realms of the ideal,
  The mist-clad land where genius' will is law.

A thousand fairies throng the wood-glades, white
  Beneath the rays of an enchanted moon;
Their elfin cohorts flash upon our sight,
  Armoured in gems that mock the glittering noon.

At music's summons Oberon's snowy steed
  Tramples the clover, jingling silver reins:
When music sounds, an unseen world gives heed;
  Its starlight waxes as our sunlight wanes.

While music sounds, what heart can ever doubt
  That life eternal waits beyond the tomb?
For music shuts cold slow-foot reason out,
  And what our souls desire our souls assume.

While music sounds, no barrier to our hope
   Looms dark and threatening on the heavenward way,
For music gives the glad soul boundless scope
   And points beyond the night to endless day.

Religion owes to music all its power :
   In man's form Jesus on the pale earth trod,
But music round him made the pale earth flower
   And changed the mortal man to deathless God.

Death conquered life ?   Nay, music's eager heart
   Repels the thought with everlasting scorn,
And with the sunlight of triumphant Art
   Transmutes to stainless gold the crown of thorn !

The Christian Church through music scales the skies :
   The humblest chapel built where wild waves foam
On Cornish rocks, or where Welsh mountains rise,
   Through music conquers, even as mighty Rome.

And love through music conquers—when we hear
   The haunting magic of some wondrous tune,
Lost loves on golden wings come glimmering near
   And life's December is as passion's June.

Dark eyes we never thought to see again
   In life shine forth, and speechless joys are won :
Music can crowd with life death's ghostly plain
   And make night's dreams more cogent than the sun.

Words—even Shakespeare's words—must sometimes fail,
   But music never fails : where man has trod
It follows, gathering up life's tragic tale,
   Blending with man's the language of a god.

And this immortal tongue is yours, O friend !
    While I must labour through the straits of rhyme
And on my course a world of thought expend,
    Your Art is subject not to space or time.

To you the lover, yearning to express
    Fancies that ravish, eager thoughts that thrill,
Must turn ; demanding love's own voice, no less,
    He finds your music's cadence tenderer still.

Demanding passion's voice and soul of fire,
    He finds your music equal to his theme ;
Strong as deep love's illimitable desire,
    Sweet as love's truth, and ardent as its dream.

Demanding that love's sadness shall prevail
    And that love's temple change into a tomb,
Still can your varying music tell the tale
    Of deepening agony and starless gloom.

To you for many a year will poets turn ;
    Through you their thought that flagged wins timeless wings :
Eyes soften at your strain, and men's hearts burn
    To whom in vain the unaided poet sings.

When pen betrays and silent paper wrongs
    The poet, stealing witchery from his strain,
Your touch brings victory ; yes, to you belongs
    The triumph, and to him the priceless gain.

Envious am I, stern fetters we must wear—
    What grim restraints the laws of verse impose !
A flower described is only half as fair,
    But music adds a fragrance to the rose.

And when across the heart life's tempest roars
  And desolation's trumpet-blast is blown,
Music can catch the clash of echoing shores
  And make the night-wind's melody its own.

If I could speak the thoughts that in my brain
  Struggle imprisoned, if on music's sea
I once could launch forth, sail that stormy main,
  If speech and music wedded once might be,

Then, then indeed, I might shake off time's yoke,
  Upon my brow the deathless stars might gleam :
Alas, what poet ever fully spoke
  The mastering thought that held him like a dream ?

PREFACE.

MUCH has been written and said of late as
to the wrongs endured by woman for ages
at the hands of man. She has been represented
as a slave : man as a pitiless and insatiable master.

It is true that woman is a slave. But man also
is a slave—man and woman, in fact, are fellow-
slaves ; chained to one another in the huge world-
galleys they have for centuries been working out—
let us hope, their redemption—but, at any rate,
their doom.

If man is woman's master, he is also—he has always been — her thrall. If woman is man's chattel, she is also—she will ever be—his queen. While he wins world-empires by the sword, she by passion wins (and retains) a mightier empire,—the empire of man's own heart. Was Cleopatra slave to Antony and Cæsar? Would it not be truer to say that Antony and Cæsar were the slaves?

Moreover, as I just now hinted, man and woman are fellow-slaves. They are slaves not only to each other: they are also fettered—sometimes even crushed—by a still more remorseless slavery, the slavery of Fate or of God. By this I mean that both woman and man—queen and king to one another in one aspect, slaves each of each in another aspect—are simply agents of the immense Cosmic Power which has worked through them from the very earliest dawn of sex, giving birth to every virtue, necessitating every crime, forceful in every dagger-stroke, passionate in every kiss, and which Power we are compelled, whether with or without reluctance, to recognise as irresistible and to pay homage to as " God."

The time for dualism in thought is rapidly passing by. The dual conception of the universe has had its day—a very extended day—but that period has come to a close, and it seems probable that by the beginning (or, at the very latest, by the middle) of the next century hardly one thoughtful person will be found who will maintain that theory. Its flash of expiring light glittered through the perverse but still luminous genius of Lawrence Oliphant. To him Satan and the Satanic host are indebted for a last brilliant but unavailing effort to muster their legions and to save their human adherents from despair.

No, it is impossible to close one's eyes to the fact that, in so far as the demonstration of the unity of the world-force is concerned, the whole field is in the hands of Science. What inferences will be drawn, during future centuries of thought and investigation, from the finally established certainty of this essential oneness of world-impulse, we may surmise but cannot fully determine. An entire reconstruction of our theory of sin will of course be necessary, and an entire restatement of the theory of the origin of evil. I should think that, within a century, it ought to be possible to write a complete natural history of sin and of goodness, and in the course of that history to explain in exhaustive detail the mystery which has hitherto been considered insoluble—the so-called mystery of the origin of evil. Moreover, the whole poetry of the next century — and of succeeding centuries—will be powerfully influenced by the death of the faith in God and Devil working in discord; by the new-born faith in God and matter working in ceaseless and majestic accord, and producing in alternate waves of rhythmical evolution the phenomena which we call good and evil, joy and sorrow, love and hatred, growth and decay. The poetic philosophy of the future will be more akin to that of Lucretius than to that of Milton.

These few words will serve clearly to explain the point of view taken in the poem which I have called *The Crucifixion of Man.* In it I have no longer regarded woman as exclusively the slave of man :

that view, the offspring of incomplete observation and of superficial analysis, will not find many adherents in the coming century. On the contrary I have endeavoured to show that woman is as often the crucifier and destroyer of the soul of man: I have traced step by step the development of sin and sorrow from seed to flower and from flower to fruit, pointing out that at no single moment in the course of the dark story is there the slightest room for the interpolation of that fancied force which we in our folly call "free-will": I have tried to make clear what all honest thinkers must now be feeling with daily increasing strength of conviction, if with a daily deepening sadness, namely that it is not man who ought to ask forgiveness of God, but rather "God" (that is, the one ultimate world-power) who, as the creator and sustainer of evil, ought to seek forgiveness of man : I have described, in minute detail and extending my observation over a lengthened period and over several lives, the "crucifixion" of man by woman and of both by God —the God embodied in physical law operating through inheritance from generation to generation with relentless rigour and ceaseless persistency.

G. B

THE CRUCIFIXION OF MAN.

PART I.

IN SUSSEX.

PART I.

IN SUSSEX.

I.

A MAN'S LETTER.

I'm cheerier now.   Your letter came
  (It helped me much) a week ago.
I never answered it, more shame ;
  I still was brooding on the blow,

That bitter blow a woman dealt :
  I still was smarting from the pain.
You saw me, witnessed what I felt,
  Yet dared to bid me, " Hope again ! "

You dared to tell me, " Life is fair :
  In time you will forget your dream ;
Feel sweetness in the summer air,
  Hear music in the mountain stream."

You told me, when we met in town,
  To fight on, to be strong and brave ;
That, if one foolish woman frown,
  Another woman's smile can save.

3

" Time can extract the sharpest sting.
　One woman has wrought you a deadly wrong ?
Will never nobler songster sing
　Now fate hath hushed one linnet's song ?

" She was a lovely woman—true ;
　I grant you all you would contend ;
Hair of the most bewitching hue,
　Eyes of seductive brown, my friend !

" And yet I'll wager in a year,
　Such are the changeful ways of man,
You'll look back, never shed a tear,
　Nay, wonder how your love began :

" Wonder you ever cared for her,
　Found witchery in her laughing gaze.
Some other woman you'll prefer ;
　Each woman has her charming ways.

" Because one gorgeous day in June
　Seems perfect, aye beyond our dream,
Will there be no more splendours soon
　When the August burning sun-rays gleam ?

" Because upon one royal day
　In summer every hour seems fair
Must human spirits put away
　Faith in new summers, and despair ?

" Or when the sun with fervour flames,
　Flashing athwart heaven's cloudy bars,

Must high hope perish ? Hope proclaims
  Beyond the sun the countless stars.

" And so with women.   Still they rise,
  Soft, blossom-like, for ever new.
Brown were thy lady's faithless eyes ?
  Love waits thee, friend, in eyes of blue.

" Much faith in God I never had,
  Yet he has done this one thing well :
He made the whole earth's future glad
  When Eve his first-born daughter fell.

" For now it is so easy—yes,
  Too easy indeed—for man to win
The first long lingering lip-caress ;
  And all things follow from that sin.

" From the first contact of the lips
  All things must follow in order due :
The fluttering flag of virtue dips,
  And soon the fair ship yields to you.

" The morning kiss leads on to those
  Whose rapture is intenser far ;
Spring's crocus is not quite the rose,
  Nor is your lamp the evening star.

" The morning kiss leads to the night's,
  When virtue with her own white hand

Draws down the blind, puts out the lights,
  And is a slave at your command."

*   *

Ah ! so you said, my cynic friend,
  In London, when I told my tale,
My passionate hope that life would end
  Since love had proved of no avail :

And here among the country lanes
  I feel there's truth in what you say ;
In losing love and hope one gains,
  For conscience passes quite away.

Love is not left, but life is left
  —What vengeance may not life contain !
Vengeance on heaven which wrought the theft
  Of love, and wrought the hopeless pain.

For vengeance is the only thing
  Now left worth living for, it seems.
Nought else is left in life ; no spring,
  No sun, no summer of lovely dreams :

No days of hope, no hours of glee,
  No golden sunshine on the hills,
No silver moonlight on the sea,
  No soft low music in the rills :

No faith in woman, nought in God :—
  I toiled for both, I served them well,

And therefore have my footsteps trod
   The endless avenues of hell.

The more I toiled, the less I win.
   The men who do not love nor pray
Win woman.   She exults in sin,
   And flings herself for nought away.

Let one man bring a ruby brooch,
   The other a life of worship true,
She'll eye the last with mute reproach,
   Say to the first, " I worship you ! "

One loves her soul, the other loves
   Her body, and the last succeeds.
One buys her bonnets, trinkets, gloves ;
   The other brings her noble deeds.

And noble deeds mean nothing much
   To woman.   She loves better far
What she can see or taste or touch ;
   Prefers a rushlight to a star.

" What *is* my soul ? " the woman says.
   She knows that she has eyes and hair ;
A tongue that flatters—and betrays ;
   Lips that can fondle—and ensnare :

But nought beyond has weight or worth
   With woman,—heaven's a dreary space !
She better loves the dear old earth,
   Her proper pleasant dwelling-place.

Heaven has its charms, but not for her ;
  Its summits loom too cold and dread.
She has the fancy to prefer
  A fire, a lover,—and a bed.

The bed must have silk curtains too ;
  The night-dress must be frilled and laced :
Chaste beauty mocks adornment—true—
  But then one is not always chaste.

Eve soon set right God's faulty thought
  And wove her leafy flounce and frill :
But if the garment had been bought,
  It would have pleased her better still !

If Jesus empty-handed came,
  And Judas brought a diamond ring,
Would woman hesitate?   She'd claim
  Knave Judas, crucify her king.

*   *

You know my story.—I was wrong
  In struggling hard, in aiming high.
'Tis better to be weak than strong :
  All talk of God's love is a lie.

The weak base selfish loveless hound
  Wins woman—this is God's wise plan ;
To let the lying cur be crowned,
  And to discrown the nobler man.

And now what vengeance? Not on those
   Who have wronged me (they are wronged as well) :
No, as my scheme of vengeance grows,
   Its blade selects the Lord of hell.

For earth is hell; aye, evermore
   The earth which holds those lovers twain
For me must with its every door
   Open on hell and hellish pain.

All things, all persons, fade away;
   Stars are but ghosts, a shade the sun :
I see two faces night and day,
   Two forms, two only,—and these are one.

          *   *

For she is one with him.   In this
   The essence of the horror lies.
Their souls are blended when they kiss :
   Their spirits mingle through the eyes.

They are not two : for ever now
   By day, by night, when her I see, —
The black hair curling o'er the brow,
   The brown eyes (full of purity !),

The forehead noble, grave and high,
   The dainty throat that I have kissed,
Lips where the whole world's roses lie,
   The blue veins on the slender wrist,—

When these I see, I see besides
  Close, closer than all speech can tell,
A man whose mocking smile derides,
  And the world darkens into hell.

           *   *

And who is Lord of hell, on whom
  The noblest vengeance can be wrought?
The Lord of pain, of death, the tomb—
  Of agony that baffles thought:

Who is the Author of these things?
  Of every pang beneath the sky?
Lord of our mortal life that brings
  With it pain's immortality:

The Power on whom man's vengeance strong
  And stern and deadly can alight;
Vengeance for unimagined wrong,
  For sin enthroned, and throneless right:

Vengeance for wrongs so grim, so deep,
  They never can be purged away:
When from the sheath man's sword shall leap,
  Whom shall its keen point pierce and slay?

Against whom shall man's kingly power
  Of grief and anger and hate arise?
Whom shall man judge in this last hour
  Of heavenly sophistries and lies?

God, surely : he who made the sun,
　The stars, the love that gives man light,
Then, just as love's own heaven was won,
　Swept all that heaven with tides of night.

　　　*　　　　　*

Enough of words—the action shows
　The manhood, not the flashing speech.
Moreover clear before me grows
　The avenging end that I must reach.

There's such a lovely girl down here,—
　The teacher at the village school.
(I shall not fall in love—don't fear !
　Once is enough to play the fool.)

Charming ! if you were in the place,
　It strikes me you and I should fight.
Charming ? divine's the word ! such grace—-
　Eyes stealing all the stars' wild light;

Hair full of night's soft darkness, lips
　Untasted yet by lips of man ;
Hands lovely to the finger-tips ;
　Complete the picture—if you can.

One day the picture shall be mine
　In all its loveliness complete :
I'll study it then, pure line by line ;
　Own it, from forehead to the feet.

—I carry home her books at night :
  We saunter through the country lanes :
She sometimes questions, " Is this right ? "
  I answer, " If my goodness gains."

For that old answer ever serves
  To lay the doubt in woman's soul.
They love to help a man who swerves
  Aside, and rein him to the goal.

Run straight—the thing's prosaic quite.
  A good girl better loves to win
A soul from darkness to the light :
  Her virtue shines against his sin.

So now this dainty teacher thinks
  That what I need she can supply.
This card I flourish, when she shrinks
  From wanderings 'neath the starry sky.

" I'm gaining so "—so I proclaim—
  " In goodness, virtue, manhood, truth :
Indeed it were a sin, a shame,
  Now to cut short your work of ruth.

" Your pitying task continue then,
  Dear Annie "—that's the name she bears :
" Make me a model among men ;
  From my cornfield snatch out the tares.

" If once a woman stooped to take
  My weary worn-out life in hand,

Who knows? I might in the ending make
    The staunchest lover in the land."

That's quite enough! We get our stroll:
    There are no more objections raised.
She talks of moonlight and the soul
    (Sometimes until I feel half dazed!)

She has read a very marvellous book—
    Sympneumata, or some such name—
And this she quotes by hook or crook,
    Now aptly, now without an aim.

A wondrous book—so I should deem.
    It solves all doubts beneath the sky:
There's one especial tender dream
    Of lovers' perfect unity.

" Dual " no more, " biune's " the word!
    No more the weary lover seeks
(The strangest dream I ever heard:
    Savours of Plato, and the Greeks).

This "sympneumatic" union serves
    Unending sweetness to provide:
Gives soul-joy, while it thrills the nerves
    —A husband, while it brings a bride.

For in far old-world realms that lay
    Beyond our trivial moon and sun,
Closed to the starlight of to-day,
    The woman and the man were one.

But Satan foiled God's primal plan :
 The "biune" form was rent in twain ;
The woman torn from out the man
 Shivering, and with a ghastly pain.

She, once divided, wandered far,
 Helpless without the enclosing form,
The man's strong shape that used to bar
 The assaults of hostile spear or storm.

He, once divided, wandered too,
 Unable now, from her apart,
To mingle as he used to do
 His with the eternal Spirit's heart.

For God inspires the soul of man,
 So runs the "sympneumatic" dream,
Through woman : thus, when life began,
 Flowed forth God's inspiration-stream.

But now the hapless halves are twain ;
 They seek each other through the years.
Man strives his long-lost bride to gain :
 She strives and seeks, with lonely tears.

And, when the long strange search is done,
 The world's redemption is at hand.
At last love's victory will be won
 And all will be as God first planned.

The severed halves again unite :
 The perfect human being is there,

Married with infinite delight ;
   And thus will end the world's despair.

. . . —So runs the dream, and so I hear
   In nightly lectures from my love.
Her words fall gently on my ear,
   Dark trees around, bright stars above.

I listen, and I vow that all
   Beyond all doubt is plain and true :
And yet such daring dreams appal
   My spirit, between me and you.

One human being ! none to seek—
   No passionate huntsmanship to show—
Romance would perish in a week,
   And with it all life's worth would go.

Or, if the loved one be a ghost,
   A spirit of the sunlit air,
One of the spotless heavenly host,
   Shall I seek my " sympneuma " there ?

Never ! I hold for love and Art
   Woman's the fittest after all.
No angel ever won man's heart :
   Man's heart was won by woman's fall.

That's my opinion. Annie thinks
   Quite otherwise—but we shall see.
I fashion all the strongest links
   Of love's chain, while she talks to me.

I listen : while I listen, slips
    The chain around her, coil on coil.
One day the sweetness of her lips
    Shall compensate for all my toil.

My letter's close—for I must go,
    I have to meet her at the school,
And you may trust me quite, you know,
    To keep both head and heart quite cool.

Good-bye, and if you're in the mood
    Write, urge your light creed's easy claims—
(Think of us sitting in the wood,
    So happy !)

                            Yours most truly,
                                    JAMES.

II.

A YOUNG GIRL'S DREAM.

Fair the world is, though the breezes of September
    O'er the moors and through the forest-alleys pass :
Though the light of burning August we remember
    Is a light for ever lost to us, alas !
Though the glory of the branches and the flowers
    Has for ever with the summer passed away,
Love is living yet within the forest-bowers
    And his heart is still as tender as in May.

Was the spring-time half as sweet to me, I wonder,
    When the pearly snowdrops peeped above the mould,
When the green buds burst their wintry sheaths asunder
    And the crocus dared to don its crown of gold—
When the sunlight flashed across the river-billows
    As the wild wind lashed them into stormy glee,
And the branches dipping in them of the willows
    Deemed they dipped their grey-green leafage in the sea ?

Was the summer half as fair with all its gleaming
    Of the crimson fuchsias near our cottage gate ?
Summer—when the stars of midnight watched me dreaming
    At the window, when I left it whispered " Wait ! "

Summer—when the rose with passion seemed to languish
  And the lily sighed her love-tale to the rose ;
When the world's heart scorned the very thought of anguish
  And its spirit was a spirit at repose.

Summer—when I wondered, wondered, looking forward,
  Who would love me, strove to picture and divine ;
Started at a fancied footstep, gazing doorward,—
  Sat in fancy, often, with his hand in mine :
Summer—when my heart knew little as I wandered
  Counting blossoms, watching butterfly and bee,
Knew so little of the love-lore that it pondered,
  Knew so little, O my lover-soul, of thee !

Was the summer half as lovely as the season
  That brings perfect love and passion to my heart ?
Let the blossoms madden at September's treason !
  Pangless, I can watch their glowing tints depart.
For my heart and all its thoughts are given over
  To my darling, and there's summer in his gaze :
Let the lily go in mourning for her lover !
  All my heart is full of dreams of summer days.

All my heart is full of dreams of love and heaven ;
  God is good to me, aye good to me indeed :
Love for teacher and for prophet he has given,
  Love for sermon and for bible and for creed.
I was lonely in the wild world, I remember,
  Lonely through the leafy balmy days of June ;
I am happy and companioned in September ;
  Envious, doubtless, is the silver lonely moon.

Envious doubtless are the sea-birds on the ocean :
    On the tossing waters where have they to rest ?
Round them stretch the waves in ceaseless angry motion,
    Where is any nook for haven or for rest ?
Envious, doubtless, are the stars i' the airy spaces ;
    Leagues they are from any loving star apart ;
Lonely sail they, leagues from love in starry faces,
    But my darling has his dwelling in my heart.

He will raise me, he will lift me by his passion
    Towards a region wholly pure and wholly fair :
We shall love with angels' love in holiest fashion,
    Yet find sweetness in the old earth's summer air.
We will visit all the old earth's sacred places
    And in every land be happy and at home,
Knit in union closer for the stranger faces ;
    Dream in Paris, pass our honeymoon in Rome.

We will wander hand in hand, with love and slowly,
    Through the cornfields and the towns of Palestine ;
Fancy that we see the eyes of Jesus holy,
    Dream we hear the voice most tender and divine.
We, the children of the dark-blue Northern ocean,
    Born in mist-land, loved and nurtured by the sea,
In the sunny East will gaze with deep emotion
    On sunstricken leafless drear Gethsemane.

All our life will be the better for the glory
    That once shone through Jesus' figure and his face ;
Better shall we understand the sweet old story
    When we see with tearful eyes the very place,

As we say, " Beneath this heaven of cloudless weather
     Wandered Jesus, here he prayed and here he spoke "—
We shall wander through the vineyards, we together,
     Where his loving heart grew weary, where it broke.

Though the beauty and the glamour have departed,
     Doubtless, from the fields and hills that Jesus saw,
Yet we'll gaze with love upon them, tender-hearted,
     And with something still within the soul of awe :
For the paths that God as perfect man hath taken
     Must for ever gleam with wonder, where he trod
Still the human heart with love and faith unshaken
     Will behold the man,—beholding him, the God.

We will trace in fancy spots he may have cherished,
     Say, " This corner of a vineyard he held dear : "
See in fancy the lone hill-side where he perished
     And the rock-tomb whence his risen voice rang clear.
" Here," we say, " the loving sad disciples wept him ;
     Here they laid his silent body to repose,
Deeming that the eternal darkness would have kept him
     Sleeping ever ; here they marvelled, when he rose."

Here our cottage has been home to me, and pleasure,
     Priceless happiness of girlhood, I have known :
To my mother been her darling, her one treasure,
     Made my father's life less weary, less alone.

—Now my life at last will leave the lowly places,
　Break to noble freedom, burst its prison bars ;
But for ever I shall love the dear lost faces,
　Love them as the golden morning loves the stars !

I will tell my husband many a simple story ;
　He will listen, for he loves me, to my tale :
Tell him of our dear old garden's summer glory,
　From my girlish dreaming draw aside the veil—
Tell him how I wandered through the hazel cover
　Dreaming of him, dreaming of him by the lake ;
How I longed to be of service to my lover,
　How I yearned to give my life-blood for his sake.

Foolish dreams, it may be,—weak and very girlish ;
　Yet they have their beauty and value, let them be !
The vast ocean is not angry, is not churlish :
　Let the river sing its ditty to the sea !
Let the river tell its quiet tales and simple
　Of the blossoms growing in the inland nooks,
Though the sea receive with hardly a surface-dimple
　All the life-throbs of a thousand eager brooks.

All my thoughts and dreams are his and he will treasure
　Touch them tenderly, transfigure one by one
All my girlish hopes and every girlish pleasure,
　As the shadowy vales are lighted by the sun.
All my friends are his—he'll make me love them better,
　Never rob me of the true heart of a friend ;
Make me faithful to each promise to the letter,
　Make me cling to father and mother to the end.

All the children shall be happy at our wedding!
   (They will miss their girlish teacher's loving rule)—
While another path and happier I am treading,
   They will tread the worn old pathway to the school;
To the same old school with honeysuckle clinging
   Round the doorway and festooning from the eaves—
I shall often hear the hymn that they are singing,
   Hear their fingers rustle through their lesson-leaves.

I shall see them trotting underneath the larches,
   See them in their scarlet tippets and their hoods,
See them enter 'neath the school-house' grey-stone arches,
   Hear their laughter in the playground of the woods:
Hear some tiny child's glad cry of sudden pleasure
   When he spies the first blue egg within the nest,
Gathers up with careful hands his turquoise-treasure,
   Shows it, full of lordly triumph, to the rest.

I shall see the first rich golden daffodilly
   Don its gorgeous glittering raiment on the bank,
Mark the snow-white wedding-garment of the lily,
   Stand again upon our brook-bridge—just a plank—
Marking, as the gentle West wind lightly winnows
   The dark leafage of the rustling alder-tree,
Half a hundred darting gleaming saucy minnows
   Make believe that they are salmon in the sea!

Then, that every thought and dream may be the sweeter,
   I will turn to him, my husband and my friend:
How the present joy will make the past completer!
   How the early days will sanctify the end!

Passing from my pleasant dream of days behind me,
   Dream of English gardens, English hill and sky,
Golden splendid Southern sunlight will remind me
   That I'm dreaming on the shores of Italy !

Then a loving kiss will bring me to my senses ;
   I must leave the children, leave them far away,
Leave them labouring over nouns and verbs and tenses,
   Leave them lonely at their labour and their play :
I must leave them, for my husband's voice is calling ;
   Leave the tender lovely dreams of early life ;
See the curtain o'er the girl's work swiftly falling—
   There's a grander mission waiting for the wife !

PART II.

IN A LONDON HOSPITAL.

PART II.

IN A LONDON HOSPITAL.

I.

A WOMAN'S CONFESSION.

First woman :—

I OFTEN wonder in this strange place
    Where the dying and dead seem one,
As my eyes meet sorrow in face after face,
    What each sad soul has done :
And I think it would ease my own sad heart
    As I lie on this hospital bed
To tell you my story, or tell you part
    —I shall tell it soon to the dead !

But I want some living soul to hear :
    We are in this ward alone,
Will you listen ? They've moved your bed quite near,—
    In the night I could hear you moan.
If you have loved, and have known love's curse,
    You may find it a help to know
That another has suffered—worse, far worse—
    Yet did not die of the blow.

         *   *

I loved him well, but I treated him ill—
  (Ah, why was it ?   Who can say ?)
I loved him truly—I love him still—
  But I flung my chance away.
Women are mad, and the maddest of all
  Is the woman who knows she is fair,
Who has love, she thinks, at her beck and call
  And can make men's souls despair.

I treated him ill, and I drove him away ;
  Then the retribution came—
Not in an hour, not in a day,
  But with fiercer than hell's hot flame.
It came with the knowledge of what I had done
  And of what my life would be :
I knew the value of what I had won
  And had squandered, woe is me !

I knew I had broken the heart of a man
  Who would gladly have died for my sake :
Blindness vanished, and light began
  Pitiless, clear, to break.
I knew I had changed his dream of bliss
  To the madness of despair ;
Kissed him, and lied as I let him kiss
  My lips and my throat and my hair.

I knew I had changed his love of heart
  To a horror fierce and grim ;
I knew God never meant we should part
  But had marked me out for him :

I knew I had sinned against love most deep,
   Most wonderful, pure and high ;
I saw one face through the mists of sleep,
   One face in the sunlit sky.

I knew I had shaken the faith of a man
   Who had served his God full well,—
Had made God's scheme like a devil's plan,
   God's heaven a starless hell.
I knew I had turned his heart to fire,
   His thoughts to a wild dark dream,—
Had changed the Lord of love to a liar—
   Ah, so it was bound to seem !

I knew that he never would grasp the whole—
   How my sad heart longed for his tread ;
That on earth he never would read my soul,
   That I should be like one dead.
I knew that the golden stars would shine
   But their glory would be dim ;
That the wind would chant love-songs to the pine,—
   They would never travel to him.

I knew I had done it—darkened the sun
   And the beautiful bright blue sea
For him, for ever—and all through one
   Who cared not a straw for me.
I knew that my darling never would know
   How the wild repentance came,
The horrible sense that never will go
   Of sin and of deep deep shame.

He had given me trust superb, complete ;
    He had found me alone and sad—
He had laboured to make my whole life sweet
    And noble and pure and glad.
He had spent a fortune—not to betray—
    To help, to uplift, and to save :
He made my life like a summer day,
    I have made his dark as the grave.

Happy we were in the wonderful hours
    While yet I had strength to be true :
The garden he gave me was bright with flowers,
    And our house was bright all through.
Bright was my bed-room, glad and bright
    The sitting-room down below :
All was perfect, a dream of delight ;
    If it could but have lasted so !

I loved him dearly, and told him so,
    But I acted a virtuous part ;
He was married—fettered and bound, you know—
    And I traded on his true heart.
I said it would ruin me, ruin me quite,
    If I gave myself away :
In his eyes I was sinless, spotless, white,
    And he would not stoop to betray.

He trusted me so !   I was housed and fed,
    One may almost say, by his hand.
He stooped like a father and kissed my head :
    Oh, the love of a man can be grand !

They talk of the glory of woman's love,
    But a man's is grander far ;
A woman's wavers,—a man's may prove
    As sure as a changeless star.

Is there any woman who ever has done
    What this man did for me ?
Held aloof from the love she had won
    For the sake of its purity ?
Was there ever a woman who stood aside
    From the love her hand might take
Lest, taking, she wounded a noble pride,
    Though, losing, her heart might break ?

Yes, his heart was broken oft I know,
    For my woman's eyes could see ;
Half I could fathom the speechless woe
    Though he thought it was hidden from me :
And I knew enough of love to feel
    When his eager lips met mine
That here was a love whose strength was steel
    Though its pureness was divine.

I was not all that he fondly thought ;
    It is so easy to sin ;
" I love you "—a kiss—and a girl's soon caught—
    That is how life's horrors begin.
When God made London, I think that he
    Peopled it straight from hell,
And his angels of light then had to flee
    From the streets we know so well !

I had had a lover in olden days—
  (But his image had grown quite dim ;
Never a mark on the lips betrays
  The kisses I won from him.
What a mercy it is that kisses sign
  On a woman's lips no mark !
They vanish at morn, like soft moonshine,
  Or the sweet stars lost in the dark.

If the loving lips we fondly raise
  To the lips we love in the end
Told tales of the errors of former days—
  But God is a dear good friend !
He kindly ordains that lips should grow
  In the moonlight into one,
Then part—that never a soul may know
  At the rising of the sun.

He wisely ordains that the wife may come
  To her husband's room at night,
Gaze in his face like a rose in bloom
  In the glare of the full sunlight,
Gaze in his face with never a qualm,
  Fondle his hair, maybe,
With the hand that parted loth from the palm
  Of the lover he cannot see.

We are made so—well, it is best we are made
  So that some of our deeds die out,
Lost in the weird deep starless shade
  Of the past, beyond all doubt :

Well for the husband, well for the wife,
  No signs on the lips betray
Last night's rapture dearer than life
  When virtue returns with the day.)

—That was hid in the far-off past,
  And I had not met James then :
It was not a love with strength to last
  When I mixed with nobler men.
It passed away, but it left me stained,
  My sense of honour was dim ;
Dim indeed—or I could not have pained
  James, and sinned against him.

For the thing that I did was mean and vile—
  I see it, I know it to-day :
I betrayed the best of men with a smile,
  As a woman's smile can betray.
He gave me passion, he brought me bliss,
  He made all earth for me fair ;
I ensnared the truest of men with a kiss,
  As a woman's kiss can ensnare.

I took his money—I took his love—
  I kissed him (I loved him too !)—
I did all this, as it were to prove
  What a pure-eyed girl can do.
I knew how he loved me, and yet I gave
  Coy pure lips to the one,
The body that he would have died to save
  To another—the wrong *was* done.

D

The horrible mad blind deed was wrought ;
  I sinned—and I liked it well ;
Keen quick pleasure can stifle thought,
  And thought to a girl is hell.
One of the reasons I cared for Will
  Was this, that he put no strain
On my mind, he let my thoughts lie still :
  He never worried my brain.

I sinned in the house James bought for me,
  In the beautiful upstairs room
Where the pictures hang of the hills and the sea ;
  Our palace became love's tomb,
The tomb of the love that came from God
  And the birth-place of despair :
I found the pathway to hell well trod—
  Plenty of girls had been there.

I held my lover close to my heart,
  I loved him because he was base :
I loved him at night and I saw him depart
  In the morning, and changed my face ;
Virginal, pure, in the afternoon
  I let James in at the door—
But my other lover came with the moon,
  And I loved the bad man more.

It was pleasant to chatter of light gay things
  To a true pure man in the day,
But to know that the golden sun had wings
  And would soon be off and away,—

That the sultry summer night would come
  And the moonlight white on the bed
And, just outside the door of the home,
  A stealthy, a watchful tread.

It was planned so well, lest the two should meet,
  For Will was a coward, I knew:
He was handsome—yes—and his lips were sweet;
  I loved him . . . and hated him too.
I hated and loved and despised him, all
  In a breath,—do you understand?
Knew that he crawled as a snake might crawl,
  And yet could have licked his hand.

That is the devilish way we are made,
  We women—by God, you say?
I think the devil made many a jade,
  Or else God did it in play!
We know that a man is a villain, yes—
  And yet if an angel came
We should turn to the villain, turn and caress
  The devil who wrought our shame.

It was hardly nobly done, I think,
  That God should have made us so.
Weighted we are, we are bound to sink,
  And to drag man with us, you know:
Weighted we are with others' sins,
  With the whole long deathful past,
For who can tell where a crime begins
  Or how long its results may last?

All that I did had been done before,
    And I only repeated it, I :—
I let sin in at a London door,
    But under the deep blue sky
Of midnight in Italy many a time
    Had the same old deed been done ;
New to me was the sense of crime,
    But not to the moon or the sun.

The sun and the moon have seen all this,
    They have witnessed it scores of times :
The stars have thrilled at sight of the kiss
    As they peeped through the elms and the limes
Here in England, or else peeped down
    Through the glistening orange-trees
In the South, or the fir-clumps dense and brown
    On the slopes of the Pyrenees.

From the day when Paris fled from Troy
    With the guilty Spartan queen
Sin has been rapture, sin has been joy—
    Aye, then it was what it had been
Through the viewless years since woman first
    Learned the subtle art to deceive,
Which means since the moment when God cursed
    The world with the gift of Eve.

We feel what the first fair woman felt
    —It is handed down in the brain—
When she found her own red soft lips melt
    On the lips she hoped to gain.

Is there a rapture known to the race
  Of women ?   Then that is ours—
As the rose of to-day has the scent and the grace
  And the colour of Eden's flowers.

That is the point—we can never escape
  From the past of the race, not one :
It will dog our steps like a ghostly shape,
  Till the life of the race is done.
Aye, worse than that, I have sometimes thought
  As I lay here, dying, alone,
That the very dead have returned and wrought
  In our world dark deeds of their own.

There are women who never could get enough
  In this world, it seemed, of sin ;
The road to the golden gate was rough
  And heaven was hard to win,
So they swerved aside—the thing may be—
  And returned to the old glad earth,
And they laughed again on the old blue sea
  And the green hills heard their mirth.

But, ghostly beings, they could not quite
  Inherit the earth once more :
They flashed out pale as the sea-foam white
  Upon many a starlit shore ;
They wandered under the summer moon,
  And they revelled once more in the breath
Of the live pure flowers of the fields of June
  And they strove to forget their death.

But it was not enough to ease their pain
  Fay-like from the tulip's cup
To gather bright beads and jewels of rain
  That the soft June night stored up :
It was not enough to breathe the air
  Of the bountiful same blue sea,
To find that the chestnut bloom was fair
  In May as it used to be.

They longed for the close warm grip of a man,
  And they sighed for the soft love-bed ;
In death they were as when life began,
  When they never meant to be dead :—
They longed for the sense of a man's love-touch,
  For the glitter of eyes and face,
For the passionate kiss they had prized so much
  And the wonderful old embrace.

So—it may be, for life is strange
  And all that one dreams comes true—
They gave up heaven, and took in exchange
  The sight of the deeds we do.
Horrible—yes, I have often thought
  As I lay here, lonely and sad,
That the sinful terrible deed I wrought
  May have made dark angels glad.

Horrible—yet it may be quite true
  (And our punishment lies in this)
That the sight of the sinful deeds we do
  May bring such ghosts their bliss.

We are not alone—we are compassed round
   By a vast beleaguering band
Though we see no vision, and hear no sound,
   And feel not a ghostly hand.

Yet they are there, the hosts of the dead :
   The bad—for the good fly far ;
They yearn not again as of old to tread
   On the earth our wild deeds mar ;
They pass to a region pure and high,
   They enter the gates of gold,
They stoop not down from the starry sky—
   'Tis the bad ghosts we behold.

And these, I have thought, must have helped me well,
   For the scheme was Satan's plan ;
The deed that I did was conceived in hell,
   The thought came not from man :
To use the house James gave me in trust
   For a deed so base and low—
To degrade his honour, yes to the dust—
   To deal him a coward's blow —

That was not the thought of a woman's heart,
   Nor yet was it Will's design :—
Bad he was (though a great great part
   Of the blame, no doubt, was mine),
Wicked he was, and I was worse,
   But the thing, so deep was the shame,
Must have had some evil spirit to nurse
   The first dim spark to a flame.

Behind Will's form some devil stood ;
  Some devilish shape, maybe,
With dark eyes like my own and as good,
  Stood triumphing close to me :
Horrible—when we heard no tread,
  Safe from fear of surprise,
Devils of hell were close to the bed
  And followed us with their eyes.

Worse—we gave them the power to do
  In spirit the self-same thing :
Will's kisses not only thrilled me through—
  Each warm kiss served as a sting
To the lust of the ghosts, and drew them close,
  Pale weird shapes, each to each ;
A phantom-husband was there—who knows ?—
  And a phantom-bride's soft speech.

That was the depth of our sin and shame,
  That the very dead came back :
Our love was never our own to claim,
  Ghosts were close on our track.
We sinned for others—we gathered flowers
  Of sin for the ghosts to wear ;
Will made a phantom exult for hours
  When he thought he kissed my hair.

They watched our passion, and what we did
  They then had the power to achieve :
Nothing was silent, nought was hid ;
  No mortal can deceive

The cold grey ghosts who glimmering back
    Defy for a time the grave,
Seek through our veins the warmth they lack
    And the pleasure the sun once gave.

We won for ourselves a rapture ?   Nay !
    We won for the devils a boon :
We gave them what they were wont to pray
    In vain of the stars and moon.
We sinned, that they might likewise sin—
    They stole our passion's flames ;
We played and lost, that they might win ;
    We gladdened their frozen frames.

        *   *

But true pure lovers are ever alone—
    With the silent stars of the night,
With the new-born lily, the rose new-blown,
    With the great sea's large delight.
They lure to their couch no ghosts of the dead,
    No spirits about them stand ;
No true man kisses a ghost's instead
    When he kisses his lady's hand.

Their room is a palace noble and wide,
    And holy thoughts are there :
They rest in their palace, side by side,
    Safe under the starlit air.

Then they rise, and they greet the morning sun,
  And the whole world seems divine ;—
Upon earth such rapture may be won,
  But it was not Will's and mine.

Would it be a comfort now to James,
  I wonder, to know how small
To the heart he loves and the lips he claims
  Was the pleasure after all ?
He judged us both by himself, no doubt,
  So he misjudged Will and me :
In thinking, he left one factor out—
  That alters the whole, you see.

He forgot that in him the poet lay
  Latent : the poet's heart
Creates by night and creates by day,
  Ever breathing the air of Art.
He created pleasure for me and Will
  With his active poet's brain ;
He created it then—he creates it still—
  Our pleasure and his wild pain.

Where is he ? Since I received his note
  With the one grim terrible word
And the few stern phrases I know by rote
  I have never never heard.
A talk with him now would ease my pain,
  One last long quiet chat—
Why did he never write again ? .   .   .

Second woman :—

I think I can tell you that.
I have heard you speak and I understand, —
    What puzzled me once grows clear,—
I have something written in James' own hand—
    Your James—and meant for your ear.
Why did he never write ? he *did*—
    And his letter is here with me,
Safe, safe under the pillow hid,
    And presently you shall see.

It was written to me, but meant for you
    On your dying bed to hear ;
Every word of the letter's true—
    He died just that way, dear.
I found him steeped in blood on the floor,
    The letter close to his hand
—Then I loved him, and hated you far more
    Than you ever will understand.

You .   .   .   so you began the sin—
    Did ever a horror, a crime,
Without the help of a woman begin,
    From Eve's to our own wild time ?
You began it, and handed to me
    Vol. I. of the novel of pain,
That the second volume then might be
    Written by me, in the main.

And volume the third—ah ! who will write
  That volume ?   I think I can tell—
A child, now drawing a child's delight
  From a world that will change to hell ;
A child, who inherits, so they say,
  My beauty—once I was fair :
Volume the third she'll write some day,
  And death shall be hero there.

The bitter evil began with you,
  But where will it, when will it end ?
The leaven you mixed will work right t hrough
  Life after life, and extend.
Life after life will sink to hell
  Through you ; as you die, you will hear
Satan whisper, "You served me well,
  And my servant need not fear !

"Fear not, daughter ; your crime was one,
  One only, but I took heed,
And a thousand dark deeds shall be done
  In the strength of that one dark deed.
The man you taught carried on the task
  And became a teacher too—"
And who was his pupil ?   Can you ask ?
  She speaks from this bed to you.

Yes, I lovèd him—loved your James—
  Loved him, not as you deem,
Not with the love that wounds and shames,
  But with love beyond your dream.

I loved him; but all his heart was dead
    When my darling came to me :
You stole it, and sent me a stone instead,
    But revenge has come, you see.

Both of us, wrecked in the world, are here,
    You dying—I brought low—
Hope has vanished from both, that's clear ;
    Nothing is left to know—
Nothing of misery, nothing of pain,
    Save only this, as you die
To say to yourself, " I sowed the grain
    And I am the reaper, I."

But your true love's letter will tell you all—
    He was lover to both, it seems ;
Yes : *you* paved the way for my fall
    With your wanton selfish dreams !
You taught James to lie, to deceive ;
    Finely you played your part
When you taught your lover to disbelieve
    For ever in woman's heart.

Now listen, hear what your lover says ;
    It is all written down quite clear—
The long strange record of hopeless days,
    And meant, as I said, for your ear,
For he left a post-script addressed to me
    And in it he bade me seek
You—so I've searched by land and sea,
    Silent : at last I can speak !

He bade me seek you, and show you this,
　And watch your face as you read ;
Hardly glad as his live warm kiss
　Will this dark word be from the dead ;
Dark—but a love-word this was to be,
　His last love-letter, he says :
If *you* cannot read it, give it to me,
　For I know each turn and each phrase.

Though I feel at nights death's finger-touch
　There is life in me left to read,
And my voice will strengthen, maybe, much
　If it makes your false heart bleed.
—Listen ; our candle's not burnt out ;
　There is time till the nurse comes in :
" James to his sweetheart "—*you*, no doubt—
　" A story of love and of sin."

First woman :—

　Read it,—the letter was written for me :
　　He would never have written to you
　A letter of *that* length—I can see
　　That at the very first view !
　Read it : the letter will sting us both,
　　It will sting you most, it seems ;
　He gave you only a broken oath,
　　He gave me his dying dreams.

II.

A MAN'S CONFESSION

I.

ERE I plunge into the darkness, fling the gift of life away,
Yet some words my soul would utter: I who cannot love nor
    pray
  Still can lodge my final protest, still with steady nerve can dare,
With the pistol on my table and the pen within my hand,
To hurl forth a final utterance that the world will understand,
  And she too, of all fair women whom I found most fickle and
        fair.

Ere I plunge into the darkness—ere I lull this weary brain
By the cold touch of a bullet into pulseless peace again—
  Yet once more, and for the last time, some relief my soul would
        seek,
Looking Godward, looking lifeward, looking deathward, with clear
        eyes,
For I pass my sorrow onward; just the brain it is that dies,
  But my vengeance yet is living,—giant-throated, this shall speak.

Yea, though I myself be silent, yet my vengeance shall survive,
Deathless ever, active ever, wholly quenchless, wholly alive;
  I shall still impress the living, bursting through death's prison
        bars:

I shall leave the cold dead resting in their dark inactive graves ;
I shall flash along the lightning, I shall thunder through the
waves,
  I shall shine amid the sunlight, I shall glitter through the
  stars !

Though men struggle to forget me, they shall not forget me—nay,
My strong influence in the wide world shall be greater day by
day
  For I leave my curse on all things, and a curse can work its
  will
When a blessing would be powerless in this world of piteous pain,
Would sink down in the dark waters, never seen to rise again
  — When love's last star is extinguished, hate's red star shall
  burn on still.

For I leave my vengeance active in a living human frame,
Operative through a woman—thus I incarnate my aim—
  For our child shall grow to beauty, and shall carry on the
  crime :
When you listened to my love-suit, you conspired to take away
All the starlight from the darkness, all the sunlight from the day,
  Aye, to make the whole world sadder through unmeasured
  lapse of time.

To our child you have given your beauty : to our child I give my
brain,—
All the sense of wrong within it, all the throbbing sense of pain ;
  She shall wreak a noble vengeance on the world of men and
  things :

As her beauty ever ripens, as it blossoms like a rose,
So, be sure, a dead man's vengeance in the world he has quitted
grows,
Ripens into perfect blossom, spreads yet wider steadier wings.

Where the father's hand is powerless, there the daughter's hand
can smite,
For the one bears keen sword-anger, but the other brings delight:
When the strong men quailed at Samson, then Delilah brought
him low,
And when Sisera went trampling o'er pale thousands in his day,
When nor sword nor lance could reach him, nor could warriors'
curses stay,
Just a nail and hammer slew him, and a woman struck the
blow.

So our daughter's hand most tender, when she grows to riper
years,
Shall add more of pain and sorrow than a host of swords and
spears
Ever added, to the total of the world's vast sum of grief:
As through her its sorrow deepens, as through her its pain-pangs
grow,
Fear not—I shall be recipient of the rapture, I shall know—
Through my ghostly veins will ripple a large current of relief.

* *

Now to tell you—ere I enter the eternal realm of night—
All my story, all that happened in the regions of the light,
For this world, they say, is sunlit, though the sun for me grew
dim :

I would tell you just what happened, that your woman's soul may
    see
Why I chose you for a scape-goat, why the very heart of me
    Changed from hope to hopeless horror, and from love to hatred
      grim.

Unto you I was as Satan? I had been as Christ to one.
I spread darkness round your footpath? I had been as stars and
    sun
    To another: I had loved her, but had sworn not to degrade.
I was married, I was fettered, but I swore my love should be
If that love were full of passion, full yet more of purity;
    Ours should be the grandest love-song Love the poet ever
      made.

Ours should be the love of angels—love of soul, with nothing
    base,
Love that craved the kiss of sunlight, and could look God in the
    face;
    What man's past had failed in doing, we two lovers would
      achieve:
I by perfect noble passion would redeem the race of man;
She by tender perfect passion stay the curse that first began
    When love changed to lower feeling in the trembling heart of
      Eve.

We were helpers of the future, we were love's strong pioneers
Sent to open out a pathway for the use of future years
    Through the thickets of wild passion, and love's darkling lowe
      deeps;

Sent to mankind with this message—" Lo ! one pair of lovers, one,
Climbs at last from old-world darkness towards the fair light of the sun,
  Dares at last, alone it may be, to attempt love's loftier steeps."

Ah ! those steeps of lofty passion, we would climb them hand in hand :
Though no frail foot dared to follow, though no soul should understand,
  We would carry out the Ideal,—here at last on earth should be
One immense love such as Jesus, had he gazed in woman's eyes
With a heart that throbbed with passion, would have brought her from the skies,
  Full of fathomless far sunlight, stolen from eternity.

Ours should be the perfect union ; yes, the touch of lip or hand,
Mortal, meant immortal union in some unseen heavenly land
  Where the God who first designed us would accomplish all things well :
Every joy was but precursor of delights more tender far
—As the one sweet silver vessel which we call the evening star
  Is the first of a flotilla vaster far than tongue can tell.

So I dreamed—and then in action strove to carry out the thing ;
Toiled to fill her life with sunshine, made her garden in the spring
  Golden with the sunny crocus, rich in summer with the rose ;

Made her house a fairy palace,—oh ! the dainty things we bought,
And each dainty gift the product of some special loving
     thought—
  Oh ! through giving, not receiving, a strong man's pure passion
     grows.

Did a finger ache ? I sorrowed. Did she sigh ? I was in grief.
Was the trouble real or fancied ? Heaven and earth for her
     relief
  I would move, past words delighted when her smile flashed
     forth again,
For of all sweet smiles of women hers was loveliest, so I deemed:
All her life I shaped to beauty, day and night I only dreamed
  Of one thing—how best to shield her from the least slight
     shadow of pain.
               *   *

Then there came one day in summer—how the sun shone out
     that day !—
When my heart, for ever pondering how to please her, found a
     way :—
  We had seen, bright in a hot-house, on the afternoon before
Such a wonderful white lily,—in its London home it dreamed
Doubtless of the tropic sunshine, and of sister-flowers that
     gleamed
  White against the dark-green foliage, on some far-off tropic
     shore.

I would buy it, I would bear it down in triumph—yes, that
     night !—
To the little house in Chelsea,—in the morning pure and white
  In the flower-box at her window it should shine against the sun :

She should wake and she should find it, guess whose hand had
    placed it there,
Stirred the mould, and set it deeply with such loving thought and
    care
  —So the sudden scheme flashed through me,—and no sooner
    schemed, than done.

Off I hastened—bought the lily—and that night beneath the
    moon
Climbed up softly to her window, while the gentle air of June
   Breathed soft perfume round about me from the clove pinks
    and the stocks
—Standing safely on a broad limb of the shadowy chestnut-
    tree
Set the pure white lily firmly where she could not fail to see
  In the centre of the blossoms in the blue-tiled window-box.

Then I stooped one foot, descending through the chestnut's leafy
    gloom,
But . . . I stopped—a thrill shot through me . . . were
   there voices in the room? . . .
  Should I look? for through the crevice of the blind I well
    might see—
Should I look? or should I banish the dark cursed thought and
    go,
The cold cursed thought that froze me, and that blocked my
    pulses' flow?
  So I doubted, and the moment was a soul's eternity.

Then I looked—and saw quite plainly, for the gas was burning
    there
Turned half down, a woman smiling, with her neck and bosom
    bare,
    Half reclining and half sitting,—standing close beside her one,
Handsome, evil-eyed, dark-bearded—the girl's lover, that was
    plain :
Twice I looked, and still I doubted—but I did not look again,
    For I heard her say, " My darling ! " What of doubt was left
    me ? None.

                *   *

Then I felt as if all history had been leading up to this,
To the horror of their rapture, to the horror of their kiss,
    Even from the far-off shaping of the golden firstling star :
God had set the worlds in motion—in my madness, so it seemed—
Just to torture me and damn me, made the moon for this that
    gleamed
    Through the window, on their curtain leaving one long silver
    bar.

Fragrance came up from the garden,—still the roses there were
    fair,
Still the sweet heart of the summer breathed its bounty through
    the air,
    Doubtless in the houses round us slept true wives in many a
    room ;
But within me from that moment grew a darkness far more deep
Than the darkness of the mountains where the sombre storm-
    clouds sleep,
    And a depth of horror deeper than the wild sea's deepest tomb.

Daily has the horror deepened,—it has made the summer strange,
On all faces round about me stamped a darkness and a change,
  Made my thoughts unreal within me, and the world outside
    me dim :
If I see a pure sweet woman, then I mark within her face
Signs of deadly treason coming—yea, in all men I can trace
  Something of the devil's likeness, being of one sex with *him*.

Ah, true madness had been mercy ! there is madness of a kind
Worse beyond all words and sadder, though the eyes of men are
    blind
  To its agony and horror, than the madness counted such.
Can a man be sane for ever, though God's angels round him
    came
Thronging with their gifts of comfort, who in one wild flash of
    flame
  Has beheld his life's one darling slay a life's love at a touch ?

Yes, a deadlier sword of anguish passed throughout my soul that
    night,
Though the whole blue heaven above me was a maze of starry
    light
  And the earth seemed one wide altar on that balmy night of
    June,—
Yes, a keener pang shot through me than the pang the sailor
    feels
On the lonely midnight ocean, when his ship beneath him reels
  And he sees the white-lipped breakers in the pale light of the
    moon.

Figures fail one—weak are figures—for the soul it is that gives
Life its rapture and its horror ; not to every man who lives
    Comes that one grim deadly moment when the live God dis-
        appears,—
When the soul is left to travel Godless, loveless, to its doom,
With God gulfed within the darkness of a never-opening tomb
    And love buried in the blackness of the unreturning years.

*   *

Miles I wandered in my madness, hardly heeding where I went,
Till I found myself at Richmond, with the darkness well nigh
    spent ;
    All the air seemed full of triumph, for another night was done :
Clear as on the mountain-summits or the waste sea's boundless
    foam,
Pure as ever over Venice, golden as on stately Rome,
    Over sin-stained weary London rose the splendour of the sun.

II.

There it rose, the golden sun-flame, changeless since it poured its
    light
Over chaos, hurling arrows through the dark heart of the night ;
    Changeless since its fiery splendour lit the first blue surging
    deep :
Changeless since it changed the waters of the first sea into gold,
Watching over the sea-desert where no ship's sail flashed of old ;
    Changeless since it saw creation quit the depths of shoreless
    sleep.

There it shone, the mighty sun-flame, changeless ever and
　　supreme ;
Changeless since it saw the blossoms on the banks of Eden
　　gleam ;
　Changeless since the first rose loved it, since that rose's heart
　　was won—
For the rose had feared the darkness, but the darkness passed
　　away,
For the conquering sun's great passion had created glowing day,
　And it kissed the first rose, saying, " Lo ! thy bridegroom is
　　the sun."

There it beamed, the eternal sun-flame, changeless since the rivers
　　heard
In the far-off past its mandate and obeyed the solar word,
　Leaping down the craggy mountains, each with laughter on its
　　tongue :
Changeless since the primal forest with its wilderness of boughs
Felt the sun within its branches rest and revel and carouse,
　Then when Nature was a maiden, when her eyes and lips were
　　young.

There it flashed, the wondrous sun-fire, changeless since the
　　ancient days
When on woodland after woodland, silent mountains, shipless
　　bays,
　Houseless meadows, voiceless prairies, reed-swamps brown be-
　　fore and dun,

Came its light to colour all things and its giant voice to say,
" Mighty were the works of darkness, mightier am I far than
      they ;
  Rise and worship at my footstool, am not I your lord the
      sun ? "

Strong as ever, grand as ever, since the far-off wondrous day
When the first man rose to worship, as it dawned amid the grey
  Rolling vapours, and the first man knew the deadly night was
      done,—
Knew the stars were but as servants, knew the night was but a
      dream,
Knew the god of the gold arrows was the god o'er all supreme,
  Rose erect and glad to worship and to bow before the sun.

Full of peerless light for ever, changeless since the wondrous
      hour
When, while Eden all around them at his touch brake into
      flower,
  Morning saw the first fair woman and her bridegroom wholly
      one ;
While a voice from the far morning said, " Ye dreamed within
      the night,
But the stars' pale dreams are over—Now embrace beneath my
      light !
  Am not I the lord of passion, as of all things, I the sun ? "

*   *

Changeless ever, though creation since has passed before its gaze;
Not defrauded of an arrow, never baffled in its blaze,
   Though the hearts of men were broken and were bowed beneath its light:
Never dimming its full splendour, though the hearts of men were dim;
Fields where battle's thousands weltered, desperate shipwreck, murder grim,
   What were these unto the sun's heart? Hardly a passing shadow of night.

Morn by morn for countless ages has its glory risen the same;
Still it swallows the wild darkness in its torrid gulf of flame;
   Still the eternal sun is victor, still it triumphs in its might:
Taking over from the darkness all its sorrow, all its dreams,
Still it mocks them with its sunlight,—as it mocks the starry gleams,
   Till the trembling star-ships founder in the ocean of its light.

And that morning over London, as I stood on Richmond Hill,
I could see the great sun rising—but the darkness' horror still
   Bore my heart down, even deadlier for the splendour of its light.
What had happened in the darkness? Could the pure and lordly sun
Take no umbrage at the foulness of the deed that had been done?
   Was he heedless of the horrors, the adulteries, of the night?

Yes, he poured his golden glory over houses, towers, and trees :
Through the foliage round about me sighed a gentle summer
　　　breeze :
　　One would think in all God's kingdom there were no such
　　　thing as night !
At my feet the grasses quivered, and the daisies on the bank
Seemed to whisper, " Lo ! he rises, grander far than when he
　　　sank ;
　　Virgin are we for the sun's kiss, see our robes of snowy white !"

Far away the river glittered, bright beneath the morning sun ;
It was flowing straight towards London, where the deadly deed
　　　was done
　　Which had made for me the darkness wholly victor over light,—
Flowing onward, ever onward, never faltering in its flow :
Though the hearts of men are broken, though our hopes may
　　　fade and go,
　　Never one blue ripple pauses in its ocean-seeking flight.

River, sun, they both are heartless—though a million sins were
　　　done
Doubtless last night in the city, does it matter to the sun ?
　　Is the sun's pure virgin lustre marred by foulness of the
　　　night ?
Is the sun one whit less joyous, as he shakes his golden hair,
Laughing, loose upon the tide-stream of the sinless morning air,
　　In that murder's face is quailing from before his piercing light ?

In the night, in London's darkness, maybe murder has been
  done ;
Lo ! a body, gashed and bleeding, prostrate lies before the sun ;
 'Tis the body of a woman, hacked to pieces in the night :
But the sun smiles at the windows of the live ones just the same,
Glitters on the happy bridegroom, cheers the agéd with his flame,
 Greets the swans upon the water with a flash of loving light.

Oh ! of all things dark and deadly is there, tell me, is there one
Quite so dark and quite so deadly as the brightness of the sun,
 Sent to tell us that all evil has for ever taken flight ?
—This it *should* tell—but it tells us that for ever evil reigns,
That for ever and for ever sin's red dripping dagger stains
 Even the glory of the sunrise with its streaks of lurid light.

This it tells us—that in London, when the empire of the sun
Ceases, then the darkling empire of some devil is begun,
 Till the moon grows pale for horror and the stars give little
  light :
Was there ever horror deadlier than the horror that has changed
All my soul into a furnace full of hell-fire, and estranged
 All my being, yes for ever, from the faith in God and right ?

Now the glory of the sunlight, heightening ever, maybe falls
On the house wherein I left them—now it lights their bed-room
  walls
 And they wake; not knowing death's hand was so near them in
  the night :

For the hand of love is death's hand, when the deadly deed is
  done
That in one man's heart for evermore extinguishes the sun
 And for evermore must poison even the sources of the light.

Ah ! they knew not—little matter—let them wake and smile and
  kiss
In the very room I gave her—let them seek a moment's bliss,
 Even one wild other moment at the ending of the night !
Well it was to leave them living ; it is life that must repay,
And their future bears a dagger, since I threw my own away,
 And made over into Fate's hand mine, the lover's final right.

Let them wake, and let him leave her—let her gently then begin
To forget him for a moment and to turn her thoughts from sin,
 Making ready to receive me, when some hours have winged
  their flight :
Let it be—she will seem lovelier in the fragrant afternoon
Of this lovely month of sinless spotless balmy perfect June
 For the kisses of her lover and the pleasures of the night.

In the afternoon she expects me,—she would let me enter there ;
She would let me bend and kiss her, kiss her throat and raven
  hair ;
 On her cheeks no blush would mantle (Did her cheeks blush in
  the night ?)
She would greet me even gladly, with a gladness hardly feigned ;
She would show the broken lily, sorrow at its beauty stained,
 Grieve at soils upon the petals that were once so pure and
  white.

She would tell me how she found it lying there beneath the sun,
Wondered how the stalk was broken, how the sad sad deed was
     done
—Now the sun has wholly risen, and all London basks in light :
But for me the night has fallen ; for my spirit evermore
Will be darkness over London, over mountain, sea, and shore,—
    Darkness mute and everlasting—I am lost within the night !

So I thought, in the wild anguish of that far-off summer morn
When my hope was changed to horror and my love of God to
     scorn,
    When I saw the devil victor and before him God abased.
Through the months that followed after I lived on, though I
     despaired :
Then I met you in the autumn, very lovely, raven-haired,
    Brown-eyed, girlish, lithe of figure, bright of heart and soul,
     and—chaste.

Chaste—the one word brought my vengeance, clear at last, before
     my sight.
Of one sex, you, with the sinner, she who in one single night
    Had slain God within his palace, murdered Christ behind the
     stars—
Of one sex, you, with the woman whom of all I loved alone
Might by loving me bring vengeance, might by loving me atone,
    Might let daylight through the window of my prison, atween
     the bars.

Annie—just the very name, too—just the name that I adored,
Just the name that I had worshipped, brought in prayer before
      the Lord,
   Many and many a time invoking sweetest blessings on her
      head :
Annie—you, the second Annie, should be bearer of the sin
Of the raven-haired first Annie—I would strain each nerve to win
   All your soul as she had won mine, she who left it dark and
      dead.

Could I love you? did it matter? You should love me—that
      was all !
You were good and chaste and noble (so was I once)—you
      should fall.
   I would carry out God's purpose—I, the witness of his plan.
I had watched him work in London—I could do the very same
In the country in October, I could plot a woman's shame
   Just as cunningly as he did ; there is genius, even in man !

God was far away, safeguarded—he who wrought the monstrous
      crime ;
He who wrought the woman's nature, shaping it from endless
      time,
   Working in it leaven of darkness, through unknown ancestral
      ways
Guiding down the stream of evil that should issue in the sea
Of vast horror that had driven all the manhood out of me,
   All the manhood, all the godhead, all the dreams of summer
      days.

God was far away, safeguarded by his angel-armies, there
Far above the loftiest summit, far beyond the starlit air,
   Safe, far out of reach, defiant—he who labouring in the gloom,
He who toiling, ever toiling, had amassed the ancestral force
That within one woman's nature took to-day its certain course ;
   He who built up passion's rapture, then set frenzy in its room :

He who saw my prayers mount upward, pure and snowy-winged
     and strong—
Bent in seeming to receive them, took vast trouble to prolong
   All the glory and the beauty and the splendour of my dream ;
He who watched the years of sorrow and the years of passion
     chained
And the anguish of the spirit that for love's own sake refrained,
   Far he was beyond the storm-clouds, past the farthest starry
     gleam !

Him I could not reach for ever—I could carry on his plan :
I a dwarf, a human pigmy, I a mere frail son of man,
   I could imitate his manner, I could sin as well as he :—
True he wrote in blood, the master—I could write a line in lake ;
True he slew his millions daily—here was one for me to take,
   Just one woman ; I could help him to blot out her purity.

I could do as I had been done by, I could render back to God
All the darkness of that morning when the great sun golden-shod
   Sprang up radiant over London and my soul was full of night :

                                      F

I a human weak mere trifler, I a mortal, child of time,
I could make my vengeance deathless, I could sin a sin sublime,
  I could keep one corner hell-dark, though the whole world swam
      in light.

God had changed a woman's nature, he had given a woman's
      frame
To a villain to make sport of, he had given to sin and shame
  Her my whole life's love and darling, he had led me to
      despair—
Should I shrink now, should I waver? I could make the ruin
      spread ;
I could tear the wreath of blossoms from another sinless head ;
  Lo! a heart with heaven within it—I could plant hell's horror
      there.

Was no pity left within me? No: sweet pity's soul was slain
In the darkness everlasting, in the unsounded gulf of pain,
  Far beyond the faintest comfort or the smallest gleam of light.
Pity dies of inanition, withers wholly—that is well :
Nought survives but blindest instinct, soulless craving—that is
      hell ;
  In man's soul the eternal horror, round his path the eternal
      night.

Oh! they speak of Christ's redemption and they prate about his
      woe:
Could his pity ever reach me, could he help and lift me? No.
  Far beyond the reach of Jesus, I had sunk within the deep.

Though he rose up on that vessel on the Galilean sea,
Stilled the waves and angry tempest, he would wake not now for
    me ;
  He was powerless, nought could rouse him from two thousand
    years of sleep.

He had vanished, he was helpless, lost amid the mists of time ;
God his Father stood convicted of the authorship of crime;
  Nothing right was left to lean on, nothing hopeful to believe.
From the far-off sunny morning when the red-gold apple swung
Tempting woman's lips and fancy every human action hung
  Poised in flawless chain of sequence, dating from the folly of Eve.

From the night when Adam kissed her, through the ages as they
    swept
Ever darkening ever onward as sin's turbid torrents leapt
  Down the channel of human history, not one chance had been
    for man :—
All was certain, fixed and deadly.   God the living lord of crime
Sat serene above the crime-floods, heedless, cruel, vast, sublime,
  And the bitter death of Jesus was one portion of his plan.

Every death was fixed and certain, every rose's wasted bloom,
Every human cry of horror, every tear shed at a tomb ;
  Every sword had left its scabbard at the high God's certain call :
Yes, the human will might struggle, but the end was fore-
    ordained,
Sure, inevitable, monstrous ; yes, our human swords were stained,
  But the sword of the Creator was the reddest sword of all.

And my darling in that bed-room—human hands had wrought the
    deed ?
Never ! straight from God our anguish, our pollution, must pro-
    ceed:
  He it was whose lips had kissed her and had left her beauty
    blurred ;
He it surely was—none other—who with lewd hand had seduced
Her I worshipped, her I died for,—who had seen her tresses
    loosed,
  Who had felt her warm lips moisten, who exulted when she
    erred.

Loving Jesus could not help me ; who had helped *him* when he
    died,
When he felt the cold spear traverse with its iron point his side?
  Who had leant from heaven to help him, when he murmured
    " I despair " ?
No : the truth was clear and certain.   God was helpless in the
    sky ;
Either helpless, or else wicked.   Christian creeds were just a lie.
  Not one human moan brought answer from the heights of star-
    lit air.

Clear and certain seemed the truth then,—yes, the wicked must
    succeed.
I had worshipped truth and beauty, acted up to love's own creed,
  Prayed and suffered for the woman, chained up passion for her
    sake :

What was my reward, God's answer? Just to fling her body down
For the human lustful devil to dishonour and discrown ;
 God had smiled upon the villain, let the true man's whole
  heart break.

That was justice, that was mercy, that was God's most noble
 deed—
Thus to let the wicked triumph, and the hideous wrong succeed ;
 Thus to bend at Satan's footstool, and to make the righteous
  bend.
This it was to trust Jehovah and to lean upon his word :
Surely of every faith the bible's was most amply proved absurd,
 For the Lord of heaven was hostile, or at best a feeble friend.

*   *

Many came and proffered comfort—" Lean on loving God," they
 said :
(Oh ! the horror of the mockery, for the loving God was dead ;
 He had vanished from my vision, and a Fiend ruled in his
  room !)
" Trust the deathless love of Jesus—he has suffered for our sakes,
He is surely close and helpful; when the human sad heart breaks,
 Lo ! his sun of love is shining on the outskirts of the gloom.

" He has suffered—worse than you do—he has borne our every
 pain ;
He has loved—and more than you did—he has died, and he will
 reign
 Now in endless light for ever with the Father there on high

Where each sorrow is wholly ended, where each sin is put away,
Where the night is merged for ever in the glory of the day :
   He can soften every anguish, he can soothe our every sigh.

" He, the tender-hearted Saviour, has exhausted human grief :
His most holy pain was endless—yours, a human pang, is brief ;
   In the Garden did not blood-drops from his suffering forehead
     flow ?
Is there any pang he knows not ? any wound he cannot heal ?
Take your trouble to the Saviour—he is human, he can feel :
   He has drunk the cup of anguish, he has drained the dregs of
     woe."

How the whole soul spurned the comfort, for the love of truth
     was there !
Something strong and pure and godlike through the anguish ot
     despair
   Spoke out straight and stern and solemn—"What of Jesus ?
     Could he know,
He who never felt the wonder of a woman's loving kiss,
Passion's rapture, passion's torture, passion's madness, passion's
     bliss ?
   Had he seen a woman's dagger slay his Father at a blow ?

" How could he, the gentle Jesus who ' exhausted human pain,'
Ever comprehend the madness that surged wildly through my
     brain
   When I stood and watched the sunrise on that perfect summer
     morn ?

When the sun had power to ravish all wide Nature with its light,
Not the power in one man's spirit to exterminate the night,
  All the horror and defiance, all the fierceness and the scorn.

" Had he loved in strong men's manner, had he loved with
    sweet desire
(Noble, pure as heaven—conceded !)—had his heart with passion's
    fire
  Ever flamed out and exulted, ever throbbed and ever glowed,
Had he loved in man's strong fashion, then and only then, I say,
Could his heart have apprehended what one human heart that day
  Felt of fathomless wild anguish,—had he trodden the self-same
    road.

" Ah ! if Jesus in the night-time, in the garden where his brow
Dripped with deathless holy blood-drops—so the Churches tell us
    now—
  If he, loving in man's fashion Mary, Mary Magdalene—
If he, gazing through the branches of the olive-thickets there,
Had seen Judas kiss her bosom and his hand caress her hair,
  Gazing—gazing—ever gazing—through the thickets' leafy screen :

" If he gazing, ever gazing, with eyes fastened to the spot,
Had seen Mary's sweet face changing as she swiftly there forgot,
  Spurred by force and stress of passion, all the lessons he had
    taught ;
If he gazing, ever gazing, had within the traitor's eyes
Marked the triumph of his treason and the triumph of his lies,
  Joy of triumph over Mary, joy of every lustful thought :

" If he gazing, ever gazing (God, will *my* eyes ever cease
To behold what once I gazed at, till the deep grave brings me
     peace ? ")—
  If he gazing, ever gazing, had beheld the woman bend
Kissing Judas on the forehead, and had heard the woman say,
' Jesus is my friend and teacher and I love him in the day,
  But at night I love you, darling — you are dearer than a
    friend ! '

" If he, ever gazing, listening, had with horror seen and heard
What I picture, what I speak of, then I grant you might a word
  Real and straight and clear of Jesus with some aptitude have
    rung.
No : his life was spared the horror.   Through the darkness when
    he died
Came no sense that one he worshipped would be sleeping at the
    side,
  Yes, that very night, of Judas, while upon the cross he hung.

" Not a sense that, while the starlight watched him slowly grow-
    ing pale,
While the red blood slowly stiffened round the sides of every nail,
  She he worshipped would be dreaming, not of heavenly life
    begun,
Only of the traitor's kisses—that the morning would disclose
Jesus dead upon the gibbet, Mary blushing as a rose
  Blushes at the morning message of the warm lips of the sun."

Others brought me other comfort—comfort—comfort of a kind!
Saying, " God is very loving, though the eyes of man are blind ;
  In the flesh she has erred against you, in the body she has
    sinned,
But the soul is safe for ever ; stately, queenly, virgin-pure,
This in heaven will surely wait you, so you struggle and endure :
  All her real self she will give you "—but such words passed
    like the wind.

" As a spirit she will love you, as an angel very fair
She will wait beyond the sunset, or within the bright blue air " :—
  Could that help me ? could that lift me ? could that stay the
    stroke of doom ?
If she gave me all her beauty in the life beyond the grave
Would that change the fact of horror that on earth she freely gave
  To a villain all her sweetness, all her pure soft earthly bloom ?

What is soul, and what is spirit ?   No, the villain after all
Wins the beauty of the woman, is exalted by her fall ;
  He obtains what he has toiled for, his reward is large and
    grand.
Woman gives him what he longs for,—gives the villain his delight
Through the sweet wild frenzied moments of the starlit summer
    night :
  Judas kisses where he pleases—Jesus may but kiss her hand.

Yes : the villain is the victor.   If through centuries of pain,
She an angel, I an angel, I may win her, still 'tis plain
  Then there will be something wanting, somewhat even then
    amiss.

Still the angel is the loser, and the selfish soul that sins,
Wastes, destroys, defiles, dishonours, is the happy soul who wins :
   The good shepherd wins affection, but the robber wins the
     kiss.
             *   *

So I sinned—with noble fulness—took you wholly to my heart ;
Used, to conquer you and win you, all love's boundless ceaseless
     art—
   Love and passion simulated, for my power of love was gone :—
Won the prize methinks the sooner, being in earnest now no
     more ;
When a man's too much in earnest, on himself he shuts the door ;
   Let his passion seem nigh setting—soon will woman's passion
     dawn !

Then I felt, deep in my spirit, when the sweet strange sin was
     done,
What the dim woods feel in autumn at the swift touch of the
     sun,—
   Something radiant, something sun-bright, seemed to flash along
     my soul :
For my soul had changed its posture—sin no longer seemed the
     same ;
Woman now was not an angel, but a tigress-heart to tame ;
   Man was hunter, no more lover, and hell's portal was the goal.

There was rapture in the darkness, there was glory now in crime ;
Aye, the deadlier now the sinning, by so much the more sublime
   Did it seem to one soul-maddened, spirit-frenzied and dis-
     traught :—

All the sins of all the nations were one sin within my brain :
Having ruined you and wrecked you, what a victory I should
    gain !
  All the Roman emperors' passions would clink glasses in my
    thought.

All the crimes of ancient Venice, where within the summer gloom
On one side an arras waited in the glory of her bloom
  Often, moulded so divinely, some sweet woman wondrous fair,
On the other side the dagger that should curtly with its gleam
Veto kisses, cool caresses, and bring death into the dream,
  Leaving just a stiff dead body on the marble palace-stair—

All the crimes of ancient Venice, where one knew not what might
    be,
Beauty's kiss, or coward's stiletto,—then a plunge within the sea
  Of a corpse at sullen midnight,—or again at perfect morn
Glances full of eager passion from dark eyes of lovely light,
Love begotten in the sunshine and accomplished in the night,
  Or a cast-off lover poisoned, when love changes into scorn—

All the old Italian love-crimes, all, I now should understand :
See Lucretia Borgia waiting with the poison in her hand ;
  Feel the rapture in my spirit that a thousand lovers felt ;
Goodness surely had its glory—sin was full of rapture too,
And that rapture I would fathom. Just as goodness once I knew,
  So I now would know its converse—let the cards be freshly
    dealt !

Yes, of all the prizes waiting, all the soul of man can win,
Is there any prize so noble as the prize they call a sin?
  Even the pureness of a woman for the immense unspoken
    prize:
Her to chase and her to conquer—her to tempt sweet day by day,
Till at last with rush of rapture all her soul she flings away
  And you know yourself victorious by the hunger in her eyes.

If God kept this prize from Jesus, yet he has another son
And an elder, even Satan, and he loves him—though we shun
  In our timid folly Satan, yet God loves him passing well:
Jesus is the younger only; on the elder God bestows
Not the lily, not the snowdrop, but the fiery-glowing rose,
  Even woman—born that Satan might decoy her into hell.

God gave empire unto Jesus, many a rapture vast and grand,
Made him ruler of the nations, lord of many a lovely land,
  Him the ages still shall worship, to the very end of time;
But to Satan God gave rapture far diviner even than this—
Woman's soul and woman's body, woman's worship, woman's
    kiss:
  Jesus wins the worn-out beauties, Satan wins them in their
    prime.

*   *

—Then another thought. 'Twas something, I a mortal, I so
    small,
Still to feel that I could wrestle with the living Lord of all;
  That in me the weak blind mortal there was somewhat
    strangely strong:

Just a verse or two, a stanza, of my poem, it might be
(Even as you hear a gull's cry through the storm-wind and the sea)
   Might be heard for all God's chanting, might outsound the
      Eternal's song.

I, confused, defeated, battered, wrecked and ruined — I, dis-
      traught,
Still maintained intact within me one indomitable thought,
   Even the thought that where was justice there was heaven,
      and where were lies
There was hell and there was Satan : aye, though Satan still
      might pose
As a God within the Churches, with a surplice like the snows
   And his hands upon the thunder and the fire-bolts of the skies.

I could dwell within the forest of my dark thoughts, in the cave
Of mine anguish, silent, lonely as the lone rock in the wave :—
   Though God flashed the stars like torches all across the
      midnight air,
I could darken still my cavern—or could bid my lantern shine
Unextinguished for his starlight ; cave and lantern both were
      mine,
   Mine the majesty of sorrow, mine the kinghood of despair.

*   *

That is all—my heart seems easier—that is all I have to say ;
Life is strange—I cannot right it save by flinging life away
   As a man's stern strong last protest, as a man's firm clear appeal

To the Power that lies behind God, if such Power indeed there be,
Even as the mightier storm-wind is behind the mightiest sea—
　　To the Power that solves the secrets that the viewless years
　　　　conceal.

Now I pass into the darkness.　Will the darkness of death's
　　　　night
Ever open out before me, and reveal a wondrous light ?
　　Shall I cast my burden from me, as the sun casts off night's
　　　　gloom ?
Truly I know not, but I enter the vast darkness without fear :
Not one star is left to light me through life's utter blackness here ;
　　Have the stars, maybe, migrated to the skies beyond the tomb ?

Second woman :—

　　　　She's quiet—the candle's quite burnt out—
　　　　　　The moon falls soft on her face ;
　　　　Is she living still ?　.　.　.　I almost doubt　.　.　.
　　　　　　She must once have had beauty, grace.
　　　　I can see the charm that drew James on,
　　　　　　I can understand her fall :
　　　　If she looked like that when the moonlight shone,
　　　　　　I can understand it all !

PART III.

THE STORY

OF THE

LIFE OF CALEB SMITH

THE METHODIST MINISTER,

TOLD BY HIMSELF.

THE STORY

OF THE

LIFE OF CALEB SMITH

THE METHODIST MINISTER,

TOLD BY HIMSELF.

WHAT a change from London, drearier as the hot days hotter grew,
To the silent bay in Cornwall, to the calm sea's ceaseless blue,
To the breeze from off the moorlands ! What a change for her
    and me
From the hospital in London to the hospice of the sea !

—Living quietly down in Cornwall with my mother, we alone,
Having nothing of a week-day we could call our very own
(On the Sabbath I was busy with the chapel-service, quite,
Busy from the early morning till the stars shone out at night)—

Having nothing of a week-day we could care for just as *ours*,
Save the fuchsias in the window—what to living hearts are
    flowers ?

I had brought away from London a small girlish flower-bud dropt
From some heavenly hand, we fancied, for our lone hearts to
    adopt.

She was daughter of a teacher—in a village school *she* had taught,
But some handsome *roué* from London whom Fate's reckless guid-
    ance brought
To her peaceful home in Sussex taught her love, and taught her
    well,
For he found her safe in heaven, but he left her lost in hell.

That was dark-eyed Annie's mother—through the round of sin and
    shame
She had passed when he forsook her—to the lowest deep she
    came
Till the hospital received her, and I found her lying there,
Just a mournful wreck of beauty, once a woman strangely fair.

I had taken a friend's sad duty, taken his mission for the day,
Just to visit these poor outcasts, and to speak to them, and pray ;
So it happened that I saw her,—heard her pale sad lips impart
Just an every day sad story, merely of one more broken heart.

So it happened, a while later, when the mother's fate was sealed
And the gateways of the darkness at her frail touch 'gan to yield,
That I promised on her death-bed that my mother and I would
    take
Her small darling child, and rear it with all kindness for her sake.

*   *

Down in sunny quiet Cornwall, as the months and years sped on,
First she grew to girlish beauty,—then a tenderer sweetness shone
In her eyes, her figure rounded.   Which is loveliest in a rose?
Its coy beauty when it's budding, or its splendour when it blows?

Hardly tongue of man can answer—hardly tongue of man could
   tell
Which was loveliest, childish Annie, at whose feet the bright leaves
   fell
In the autumn, one might fancy, just to hear the laugh that rang
As her childish steps pursued them, or the girl whose sweet voice
   sang.

Yes: for ever she was singing, with a voice that mocked the birds,
Putting wonderful new sweetness into even the homeliest words;
Singing to the morning breezes, singing to the midday sun,
Singing to the stars that listened when the summer day was done

Ah ! how often have I watching seen some stalwart sailor stand
Silent in the narrow roadway, with his nets in sunburnt hand,
Listening as she sang some love-song, with his dark eyes full of
   tears :
Leagues away the sweet voice took him, to far other lands and
   years.

And I've seen a mother listening, with sad eager eyes and deep,
To a wild song of the storm-wind, and I've seen her turn and
   weep,
For she thought—her eyes disclosed it—all her heart was plain to
   me—
Of some sailor-boy, the offering of the storm-wind to the sea.

And the younger women listened, as the girl's pure sweet voice
    rang,
And I knew their hearts were hanging on each simple word she
    sang :
They were dreaming of their sweethearts, of the lads they loved
    so well,
And to each the song spoke gently, with its own strange tale to
    tell.

So the days and years fled past us, and I rendered thanks and
    praise
To the good God who had sent us such a help for lonely days.
We should nevermore be lonely. Could one's heart ache when
    she smiled ?
Was she not our own for ever ? Was the girl not as the child ?

          *   *

But a mighty change came o'er me, for one lovely August morn
Off we started, I and Annie, and we walked through fields of corn,
Over many a breezy hill-top, while the sea beneath us shone,
Flashed its sapphires in the sunlight, as it smiled up at the sun.

There the fishing-boats were lying which in winter-time had dashed
Through the blinding whirling snow-storms, while the thunderous
    great waves crashed
Over gunwale, over bulwark ; there they rested like the boats
On some silent summer river, where the untrembling lily floats.

Oh, the splendour of that morning ! How it all comes back to
    me !
The sweet scent from cottage gardens, and the fresh scent from
    the sea :

Endless perfect radiant sunlight poured on meadow, hill, and
  plain ;
For one hour the calm of Eden seemed to rest on earth again.

Hard it was, most hard, to fancy that the golden fields of corn
Ever by the winds of autumn had been smitten and lashed and
  torn :
Hard it was before the vision to call up the breakers white,
Filling all the bay in winter with their thunder day and night.

Perfect peace upon the waters—now the soft breeze sang a psalm;
The old trumpet-throated storm-wind had subsided into calm.
Perfect peace upon the moorland—dark the silent fir-clumps
  gleamed,
And within them the wood-pigeon murmured gently as she
  dreamed.

Wondrous light upon the town too ; as we clambered up the hill
All the houses down below us seemed asleep, they were so still :
Little quiet whitewashed houses—all was peace in Newlyn town ;
Peace and rest and golden sunlight, so it seemed as we looked
  down.

Such a sense there was in Nature, past the reach of words or Art,
Of a silent something waiting, of a loving spirit and heart.
I could almost feel the sweetness of a kiss within the air :
Almost catch within the cornfields the quick flash of golden hair.

Never till that very morning had the strange sense come to me
Of a life behind all Nature, of a soul within the sea ;

Of a glory past expression, of a rapture to be won
From the silent heart of Nature, of a secret in the sun.

As we passed the cottage gardens where in sunlit soft repose
Gleamed the giant climbing fuchsias, the geranium and the rose,
I could see and love the blossoms, but the blossoms' selves were
    nought :
There was something hid behind them, even a sweet creative
    Thought.

There was then a soul in Nature—all was soulless, dark, no more;
There was woman's silvery laughter in the wave-pulse on the
    shore :
There was mystic meaning hidden in the dark-blue depth of air ;
Far within the being of Nature was a Presence yet more fair.

And this Presence, turning meward, filled the land and filled the
    sky
With a glory vast and solemn, with a rapture pure and high :
I could reach the sacred Presence, I could worship at its shrine ;
More—my very soul could claim it, I could murmur, " Thou art
    mine ! "

There was something, deep in Nature—something sweet to be
    attained ;
Heights of holy love to reach to, sacred friendship to be gained :
Something strange that, ever eluding mortal grasp and touch of
    hand,
Seemed to whisper, "Yet I love you—yet I smile and under-
    stand !

" I am weary of the cornfields, I am weary of the air
Full of scents of radiant summer, I am weary of the fair
Starlit night that follows sunset, I am weary of the tides
Laving lonely coasts of granite and lone coral-islands' sides ;

" I am weary of the sunrise over mountains lone and vast,
I am weary of dead ages, I am weary of my past ;
I am weary of the worship of the star-hosts as they wheel,
As they dress their ranks obedient to the bugling thunder-peal ;

" I am weary : I am eager not for soulless sympathy
Of my soulless white-sailed cloud-ships as they plunge along the
    sky ;
I would see my love reflected in the human soul, my thought
In the brain that I for ages past man's lengthiest dream have
    wrought."

So the loving sweet voice whispered—then it changed to mocking
    mirth,
Saying, " Yet I dwell in dreamland, I am part not of the earth :
Never human soul shall reach me till the course of time is run,
For I dwell beyond the sunset, and I dwell beyond the sun.

" Mightiest poets all have sought me—they have found me pass-
    ing fair ;
They have sung the glittering radiance of the morning in my
    hair :
Every soul has thought to claim me—each has seen within my
    eyes,
When he dreamed that he possessed me, the first virgin tear-drops
    rise.

"Byron thought our wedding-chamber was the palace of the sea ;
Wordsworth sought me on the mountains, Shelley sought in
     Italy,
And the lips of Keats my lover on my own lips seemed to close
So he fancied in the violet, so he felt within the rose.

"What the Christians find in Jesus, other loving souls have
     found
In the golden light of morning, in the rushing rivers' sound :
Yes, a godhead is in Nature, a divinity in me ;
Once God thundered upon Sinai—now he thunders through the
     sea !

"Now he thunders on your mountains—when your mighty poet
     heard
Jura thunder, he was listening just as surely to the word
Of Jehovah as was Moses in the desert lone and grim :
Ever in Nature ye may find me, though to-day ye find not him.

"Though the Jewish God has vanished, though his angry light-
     nings gleam
Down the rocky heights no longer, though his kingdom was a
     dream,
I am living, I am with you, there is majesty in me :
In the red rose there is passion—there is love within the sea."

So the sweet voice seemed to whisper, and I fancied as I heard
That a tenderer soft note sounded from the throat of every bird,—
That the lovely colour deepened in the flowers beside the road,—
That the sea's plain in the distance with a nobler radiance
     glowed :

And a wondrous sense came o'er me that for me that very day
Virgin was the spirit of Nature, that within my arms she lay
Never touched and never fondled, that she cared for me alone ;
That she deigned to love a mortal, and to draw him towards her
    throne.

Though the far primordial hill-tops and the ancient winds and
    streams
Wrought their passion into music and had brought a million
    dreams,
Though man's heart throughout the ages had paid homage at her
    shrine,
Yet that day the spirit of Nature seemed superbly, wholly, mine.

*   *

But the loving spirit of Nature had yet further gifts in store :—
Turning homeward, round the cliff-tops, as we gazed on sea and
    shore
Came the marvel of the sunset—as the sun sank to his grave
Such a flood of golden glory lighted cliff and beach and wave !

Golden glory—stainless molten glowing wonderful deep gold :
Many a sunset from those cliff-tops had I watched and loved of
    old,
Never sunset quite so perfect, never sunset so divine,—
All the stars' whole wealth of radiance in its least ray seemed to
    shine.

This was Nature's bridal raiment, thus was Nature robed for me
In this golden wedding-garment flung across the sky and sea.
All that day had Nature wooed me, but her noblest gift was
    this ;
With her soft voice she had charmed me—now she thrilled me
    with her kiss.

— That was just one August sunset ; but the glories never
    known !
Wealth of tropical strange sunsets where the weird sun sets alone
Over lonely wastes of water, or by reed-swamps dim and deep,
From his lonely labour passing to his loveless lonelier sleep !

Glory of prehistoric sunsets, when no man's eye might behold
All the Western far heaven flushing or with rose-tints or with
    gold :
When no lover whispered gently, " Though the sun beyond the
    sky
Should depart and dwell for ever, golden love would never die ! "

Sunsets it may be in star-land, countless sunsets it may be
Over starry silent oceans, many a dark-blue astral sea ;
These the spirit of Nature painting ever paints alone, apart,
Mocking human pen and pencil, with strange laughter at her
    heart.

" Would one human artist follow ? Can he pass amid the stars ?
Can he cross their golden portals ? Can he leap their harbour-
    bars ?
Lo ! I paint ten million sunsets, while he strives to understand
Just one earthly sunset colouring half a mile of sea and land.

"While the deep sea drags a vessel down beneath the tossing foam

In the heaven I mix my colours, fiery lake and magic chrome;

In the peaceful heaven above them, while the sailors shriek distraught,

I achieve a feat of sunset Turner's genius never wrought.

"Painters, poets, all have striven—all have failed to follow me

When my brush sweeps o'er the canvas of the answering sky or sea.

They may struggle, they may marvel—Nay, the flamelit sunset air

That for me breathes only triumph for man's genius breathes despair."

* *

Then the next day in the chapel, lovely summer still without,

How I preached, with what an unction! Not one single shadow of doubt

Crossed the preacher's mind that morning—all he said, to *him* was true;

So his passion reached the people and it held them spell-bound too.

I had preached to them of Jesus, I had told them of his grace;

I had drawn them moving pictures of the Saviour's grief-lined face;

I had preached to them of heaven—I had pictured to my fold

Heavenly doorways bright with jewels, heavenly mansions wrought of gold.

I had told them that the Saviour is not dead—that still he stands
With the infinite same pity in his heart and outstretched hands :
That the Father's heart is changeless ; that to every soul who
　　wills
Jesus speaks his Father's message, by our Cornish rocks and hills.

"Is there one heart in this chapel full of sadness ? " so I had
　　said ;
" Let him grasp the fact eternal that the Saviour is not dead :
He is living yet to pity, he is living to redeem—
All of real life is the Christian's, all the world's life is a dream.

" As he spake to his disciples by the Galilean sea
So he speaks to-day in Cornwall, so he speaks to you and me :
He is near us, he is with us, and he sees with pitying glance
Every suffering soul in Newlyn, every sorrow in Penzance.

" Though your boats upon the Atlantic, not on any inland lake,
Bury deep their bows in winter when the thundering great waves
　　break,
Tremble not, for he is near you—aye, the tiller is in his hand,
And it has not lost its cunning—he can steer your boat to land.

" Jesus dreads not all the Atlantic ; he is just as much at home
On your vessels, when you are blinded with the scudding sleet
　　and foam,
As on boats of humbler fashion on a sea of humbler waves
When he succoured other sailors.　Still he watches, still he
　　saves.

"Not the sea alone he conquers, all of Nature he can rule :
By his grace the water-lily buoys its white cup on the pool.
Nature is but as his servant, and beyond the sights we see
There are sights more glorious waiting, waiting in eternity.

" Past the blue waves of the ocean there are bluer waves than ours,
And the roses at your windows tell of heavenly fairer flowers :
For each passion that we conquer, for each joy that we disdain,
There are heavenly high gifts waiting, when our Master comes to
    reign.

"Comes to reign, for he will surely from the highest heaven
    descend
And all human sins and sorrows, aye the world's whole life, shall
    end :
There are many—I believe it—even now living who will see
Jesus coming in his glory, in his power and majesty.

"Oh, the flowers of earth are nothing ! oh, the loves of earth
    are nought !
Oh, the joys of earth are trifles, hardly worth a passing thought !
Earthly flowers may dread the winter, mortal sunshine yield to
    night,
I proclaim the life immortal where the Lord God is the light."

—But *that* day I preached of Nature, for the spirit of Nature
    seized
All my soul and chained and held me, and compelled me as she
    pleased :
I was thinking of the sunlight on the sea the day before—
How it glittered on the ocean, how it gleamed along the shore.

" Heaven is close, aye all around you ! " so I cried to them that
    day ;
" It is in the golden sunlight as it flashes on the bay :
Even the highest heaven is sunless when God sends, some
    summer morn,
All the sunlight he can gather to assist your fields of corn.

" Moonless, starless are the heavens, lampless is God's house on
    high
Sometimes, when the lamps immortal gleam across a mortal sky,—
And the angels seem less stately, and their gold robes seem less fair,
When the glory of God's sunlight glitters through a woman's hair.

" Woman was not made to tempt us !   Was not Christ, the God-
    child, born
Of the pure womb of a Virgin ?   Did the world's Creator scorn
Even the lowly flesh of woman ?   Was it not the great God's plan
Through the stainless heart of Mary to redeem the race of man ?

" Sacred evermore is woman, sacred is this world of ours,
For the fingers of its Maker now have plucked its humble flowers :
Sacred are its fields and valleys, and its mountain-heights sublime,
For eternity has sought us, and has kissed the lips of time.

" Now the heart of God that revelled through the years that
    baffle thought
Far in heaven 'mid heavenly splendour loves the flowers his
    earth has brought,
And a fairer light than heavenly is in sunlit Cornish skies."
Then I stepped down from the pulpit—and my eyes met Annie's
    eyes.

              *   *

Next there came a time of horror, when my soul saw nought of
light,
Wildly longed by day for Annie, then yearned heavenward through
the night ;
Till at last my thought grew clearer—I would seek the friendly
sea—
The vast loveless waves should heal me and the winds should set
me free.

Round the coast just now was sailing, ere the summer days were
spent,
The dark fleet of herring-fishers, on their Northward voyage
intent,
From Penzance to Whitby steering : I would join them once
again ;
Strangle love, the sea's strength helping—stifle love, and deaden
pain.

So I sailed with them and struggled, was victorious for awhile,
Dreamed of passionless cold sea-wastes and the white moon's
loveless smile—
Dreamed that love had never thrilled me, dreamed my heart was
wholly dead—
Till one starlit night we anchored, half the fleet, off Beachy Head.

Then there came through all the calmness of that starlit night at
sea
The full fierce storm of reaction, smiting body and soul of me :
While the stars upon the water in untroubled silence gleamed
Thus my storm-tossed troubled spirit in its starless anguish
dreamed :—

"What a peace upon the waters !   What a storm within my soul !
Through my heart the giant surges of an endless sorrow roll :
All is calm and still around me, countless stars above me shine,
And the peace of God is in them, but the travail of man is mine.

"Shall I never win God's peace now? must I bid sweet love
        depart ?
Wrench the image of a woman, and for ever, from my heart?
On the land the roses blossom, and God bending from his throne
Sends them love and sends them fragrance : I am loveless, I alone.

"Star to star sends holiest greeting,—even the sea-bird from the
        wave
Takes not back the kiss that, passing, with its swift white wing it
        gave :
But God sends a heart to love me—then he takes that heart
        from me ;
I am lonelier than the lone stars, I am lonelier than the sea.

"In the morning past the green banks in our Cornwall she wil
        go,
Through the lovely Cornish deep lanes draped with fern-fronds
        loiter slow :
Will she think of me, I wonder?   Will the fern-fronds hear her
        sigh ?
Or will all be peace and gladness like the gladness of the sky ?

"Bird to bird will softly murmur, 'This is fairy-land's pure queen
Sent to tarry here with mortals, for a season known and seen :

How the heart of man must love her?' Then the violet in
    repose
On the mossy bank will whisper, 'She is lovelier than the rose !

" ' Though I love the wild red rose-bud, she is lovelier far than
    this !'
Then the wild red rose will murmur, 'Though I love the violet's
    kiss
There's a softer sweet kiss waiting, there's a sweeter mouth than
    hers ;
Aye, a noble kiss more luscious than the flower-kiss of the furze.

" ' I am only a hedge-row blossom—I would die in her embrace
Were I but a man to love her, were I in her lover's place !
I would bring the whole world's emeralds, every ruby I would
    take ;
I would search the depths for diamonds, sack the gold-fields for
    her sake.

" ' That must be the glory of loving,' so the rose will murmur low,
' Not to rest among the hedge-leaves while the days pass, dull
    and slow,
But to ruin oneself for love's sake—ruin the world, if that may be !
Steal the stars to fill love's coffers, drag lost treasures from the
    sea.

" ' Were I but a man, my violet, were my violet but a maid,
I would lift her into sunlight, I would lift her from the shade :
I would chaffer with the angels, bring their choicest gold robes
    down ;
I would even drive a bargain with Jehovah for his crown ! '—

H

"So the wild red rose will whisper, as it were rebuking me.
Have I torn for her strange treasures from the green depths of
the sea?
Have I brought her rubies, sapphires? There are nobler jewels
above:
These I craved for, these I sought for—and my heart was closed
to love.

"O my Master, have I left you? Is there even a stronger power
In the world than that of Jesus? Is this simple snow-white
flower,
Even the flower of love that Jesus in his kingly sternness scorns,
Far more potent through its fragrance than his pale wreath
through its thorns?

"Have I after all been preaching of the life beyond the tomb,
Preaching of the heavenly blossoms, while I loved a lily in bloom
Here on earth? Have I been preaching of sunlight beyond the
skies,
Dazzled all the while with starlight, even the light in Annie's
eyes?

"Have I only dreamed of Jesus? Have I acted all the while
As if dearer far than Jesus was a girl's quick sudden smile?
Have I been content with fancies of the sinless heavenly land
While to me the heavenliest rapture would have been to kiss her
hand?

"All these years have I been traitor—yes, a traitor to my Lord?
When I thought I worshipped Jesus, it was Annie I adored:

When I thought the Spirit of Nature spoke from wave and bush
and flower,
It was Annie whom I worshipped,—she was sovereign in that
hour.

" It was not the Spirit of Nature, it was passion after all,
Just the same old pagan passion—what a hideous lapse and fall !
I had sworn to banish passion from my life—to live and die
As a preacher of the gospel, with my home beyond the sky—

" I had preached of self-denial—I was conquered, I was base,
Conquered by a girl's young laughter, by the young pure lovely
face :
Venus still alas ! was living ; I was sin-stained and defiled ;
Madly (I see) I loved the woman, while I thought I loved the
child !

" While I taught her of the next world, she was slowly teaching
me
Just what Venus taught to mortals when she sprang from out the
sea.
I was teacher—she was pupil—but the pupil was more wise ;
While I taught with pen and pencil, she was teaching with her
eyes."

So I reasoned through the night-time, but my spirit reached no
goal :
Star to star gave loving answer, but they spake not to my soul.
I was left alone and joyless 'mid the universal peace ;
" Love is born," my heart had whispered—now it whispered
" Love must cease."

*   *

But the morning came resplendent—when the summer night was
    done
All the sea flashed laughing answer to the first kiss of the sun,
And my soul flashed laughing answer to the thought that in it
    lay :
All my past life had been darkness—Now at last triumphant day !

Now at last sunrise immortal !   As I gazed across the waves
Leaping, smiling, snowy-crested, could one dream that they were
    graves ?
Never ! Where was thought of shipwreck ?   Surely shipwreck
    could be none
In a world where such blue waters laughed beneath so bright a
    sun !

All was peace and all was beauty.   Could I dream that love was
    wrong
Listening, as my whole soul listened, to the bright waves' morning
    song ?
Was not passion in the sunlight, was not passion in the sea ?
Was not passion too in God's heart, doubtless, from eternity ?

Had some souls perchance made shipwreck through their passion,
    so 'twas said ?
Yet behold the flood of sunlight flashing down on Beachy Head !
Beachy Head had seen its wreckage : Beachy Head that summer
    morn
Laughed the very thought of shipwreck 'neath its high white cliffs
    to scorn.

No : there never had been shipwreck—it was but a dream of
    pain,
And there never could be shipwreck on this sapphire sea again ;—
Never wreck of any vessel, or of any soul should be,
For God vowed it through the sunlight, and he promised through
    the sea.

All the universe was passion ; all the universe proclaimed
The pure glory of love for ever, with a million tongues un-
    shamed :
Every flower on earth proclaimed it, every wave upon the deep ;
Would God plant love's golden cornfield, then forbid man's hand
    to reap ?

Annie—yes, my love for Annie was one verse, one radiant line,
Of the universal poem written by the hand divine :
I could add one perfect stanza to the world's vast hymn of praise ;
Though the ages' joy was in it, I could add one summer day's !

I could write one passionate lyric, one small song, if heaven
    should please,
Though the Epics were Jehovah's and the vast Odes were the
    sea's ;
Though the sweetest tenderest poems bore God's signature, 'tis
    true,
Yet I, loving past expression, could strike out some music too.

So my soul won liberation : as the sun climbed higher I saw
All my future stretched before me with a throbbing sense of awe ;

All our future—yes, *our* future—for my life and hers were one,—
So God promised through the bright sea, and he sware it by the
sun.

What if many a soul, defeated, down had sunk beside the way?
She and I would be victorious! love at last should have its day!
Were a thousand women traitors, yet one woman (sang the sea)
Would be loyal and true for ever, and bring perfect love to me.

Yes, to-day creation started on its journey quite anew:
For the first time heaven was cloudless, and the sea was stainless
blue.
Though a thousand women wavered, yet one woman (said the sun)
Through all life would follow bravely—and my Annie was that
one.

I would carry out my purpose now my heart had found repose,
Would not quit my sailor comrades till their summer journey's
close:
I would watch them at their fishing; I would preach (with what a
force!)
I would let all things that summer take their old unaltered
course.

Then when they were leaving Whitby, sailing South and sailing
West
In the first days of the autumn, I would travel with the rest:
When the summer was quite over, then my summer should be-
gin;
I sailed North to lose a life's love—I would Southward sail to
win.

I would Southward sail to win her. Oh, my darling, waiting
    there,
Far in dear old magic Cornwall, joy is sometimes hard to bear!
I should find her as I left her, hear her sing that old sweet song;
Tell her—tell her how I loved her—though she knew it all along.

*   *

Why, when hopes of man are fairest, does some dark fate dash
    them down?
Does it give the Lord God pleasure first to crown us, then dis-
    crown?
—When I came again to Cornwall, with the first autumnal leaf,
Love, who had given me lordly pleasure, brought me never-dying
    grief.

She was gone—to her destruction—so they told me, when I
    came;
If she had not fallen already, she was on the road to shame:
Dazzled by the foolish glitter of a troop of acting knaves
She had joined the troop of players,—she had left our moors and
    waves.

She had left Penzance for ever—so the little letter said
That my mother grave-eyed gave me—would we think of her as
    dead?
She was weary of quiet pleasures—she remembered all we had
    done—
But the wide sweet world was waiting—there were grand crowns
    to be won!

There were crowns of fame and love-crowns, so the poor sad
    scrawl went on :
She could never rest contented here to live and die unknown ;
I must never never seek her, she would not disgrace us, no—
It was her own choice, her doing : she had freely chosen to go.

She had joined the travelling actors for a season, so she said :
That was just as a beginning—soon she would be better paid ;
She would send us wondrous presents from great London,—she
    was told
That her voice alone would bring her fabulous wealth, uncounted
    gold.

We were not to be too sorry—she would far far happier be
In the midst of wild excitement than by our grey lonely sea ;
For she needed wild excitement—it was always rest to dance,
And I knew what dull companions came to see her at Penzance.

She did *so* like jolly people ! all the actors were so bright—
Got up late and tired, that's certain, but they sat up half the
    night
Talking, singing, telling stories—and the acting was great fun ;
She liked gaslight, always, better than the ugly glaring sun.

She would like me to be sorry—just a little—for her sake ;
Sorry only just a little—did not want my heart to break :
I should doubtless soon find some one who would make me a
    better wife
(If indeed like that I loved her)—mine was not her view of life.

She was grateful, very grateful—we had always been most kind ;
We must try now to forget her, try not overmuch to mind :
When she thought of all our goodness the thought always made
  her cry,
But then crying made her eyes red—that would never do—Good-
  bye !

*   *

So the weary search began then, and for months that search went
  on :
Half through England I went seeking, silent, grim, forlorn, alone,
Past all human words despairing, with despair that mixed with
  shame,
For I knew well, if I found her, she would never be the same.

No : the damning step was taken.   Fate had tossed her on the
  sea
Of the great world, given the devil his grand opportunity :
If the devil did not seize it, he was not the devil of old,
Swaying man by lust of woman, woman's heart by lust of gold.

As the dark sad thought flashed through me, I remembered
  where he reigns,
Satan, chiefliest crowned as monarch, not as king of hills and
  plains
But as deathless lord of London—king eternal and supreme
Of the city where the gaslights on his countless armies gleam.

There, it might be, I should find her.   There for some two years
  I sought
Vainly, vainly, ever vainly—hearing nothing, finding nought ;

Till at last, one evening, entering Charing Cross to catch the
    train
I ran almost up against her—yes, her very self again.

Yes, her very self unaltered—so at first I fondly dreamed :
Nay, the light that through the dark eyes flashed and sparkled,
    shone and gleamed,
Bright and lovely, was not lovely as it used to be of old ;
Now the gaze had grown self-conscious, it might be a trifle bold.

Yet she seemed well pleased to see me and with tears the brown
    eyes filled
(Ah, for just one rapturous moment all the storm of life seemed
    stilled !)—
Then we moved away together, out of sound and sight of all ;
Much my heart fails to remember, but these wild words I re-
    call :—

" Yes, I always loved you dearly, but you would not understand
You were thinking of your preaching—you were sombre, and so
    grand !
You were thinking of the next world—I was happy, quite, in
    this—
And you dreamed of heavenly mansions, while I coveted a kiss.

"You were wrong and I was right, love—I was ready, you were
    not ;
You were writing passion's novel but mismanaging the plot :
Come with me—I want to show you that my life is glad and
    bright ;
I will love you, sad old lover, I will love you for a night.

" I will love you—yes, for nothing—that I never did before ;
I will show you all my treasures, you shall be one conquest more :
You look grave and you are solemn, but I know you love me
    well ;
When you travel back to Cornwall you shall have a tale to tell.

"You shall see my diamond earrings, and my lovely china jars
With such strange old pictures on them—one of Venus kissing
    Mars :
You shall see my blue plush curtains and my ostrich-feather fans ;
All my room is like a dream, love,—fairer far than dream of
    man's.

"Oh, you used to tell me stories of the fairies, what they did,
In their palaces immortal or their leafy coverts hid ;
But my palace is the richer and my jewels are more grand
Than the jewels of the fairies through the whole of fairy-land !

"There are blossoms everlasting in my room, they never fade ;
It is merely a small question of the florist's man well paid :
Did the fairies' blossoms glitter even in wintry hostile hours ?
That is nought ; in mid-December I can gather hot-house flowers!

"I have strawberries—yes, at Christmas—I have peaches when
    the moon
Dreads her dreary five months' journey to the purple skies of
    June :
I have everything I wish for ; if I craved for one thing more
I should surely in the morning find it set outside my door !

"That is love, you know—to gratify a woman's every whim :
That is better far than preaching of the saints and seraphim ;
Those old saints you used to preach of—how I pitied them poor
　　things,
Dragging o'er the heavenly hill-tops their gold harps and heavy
　　wings !

"I'm a saint too—some one thinks me quite a lovely perfect
　　saint :
If you knew how he adores me—and his stories are so quaint ;
Oh ! the anecdotes he tells me—(let me whisper in your ear,
He's a lord too—but be careful—not a soul must ever hear !)

"There was never girl so perfect—and he says a perfect girl
(Shall I trust you even further ? yes, I'll tell you—he's an
　　earl !)
Ought to know all sorts of stories, ought to hear all kinds of
　　things ;
Yes, I like him all the better for the funny books he brings.

"There are goody-goody stories—there are novels of intrigue—
And I read the former yawning, but the last without fatigue ;
There are wonderful French novels, full of horrors—just like
　　life—
Where the good man dreams of heaven, while the bad man steals
　　his wife.

"I get up at twelve to breakfast, and I go to bed at two ;
That seems wonderful, old lover, and disgraceful—yes, to you.

Down in Cornwall you don't labour like us Londoners at night :
When the stars and weak moon fail us, we turn on the electric
    light.

" But we're wasting time—step out now—I will show you where I
    live,
And I'll give you one night's pleasure—that's a real big boon to
    give
(All for love too, all for nothing) when the golden youth in town
Pay a brougham for a smile, dear, and a bank-note for a frown !

" For I frown upon them sometimes, and they love me just as
    well,
Stuff their bank-notes in my pocket—then I laugh and come and
    tell
My real darling, my brave lover, my kind ducky of an earl,
That he's found a faithful mistress, quite a treasure of a girl.

" Come, come quickly, for to-morrow—so he writes me—he'll
    return ;
There's one night, my friend, still left you—hasten—never look
    so stern !
Why your whole glad face should brighten with a measureless
    content
When a girl so tries to please you. You'll come with me ? "
                                  And I went.

                    *   *

Yes, my soul had been too eager; I had raised my hopes too
    high ;
I had dreamed of perfect goodness there beyond the starry sky :

I had thought that over all things reigned a God supremely pure,
That he stooped from heaven to help us—but my faith was
    premature.

I had dreamed that by his Spirit every noble deed was wrought,
That he bent from heaven inspiring every sweet unselfish
    thought,
That he bade us seek his counsel and his grace to sanctify,
Breathing round us ghostly comfort, ever watching, ever nigh.

I had dreamed that all our sorrows could be used by him to
    teach
Holy lessons worth man's learning, mysteries passing thought and
    speech ;
I had loved and I had worshipped—by the wintry Cornish foam
I had dreamed of stormless havens, of a Father and a home.

When before the grey-green breakers, plunging wildly through
    the waves,
Fled the fishing-boats in winter, while the hoarse wind through
    the caves
And the crags and coigns of granite swept with horror in its
    roar,
I had dreamed of heavenly sunshine shed along a waveless shore.

I had loved the bearded seamen—I had preached to them of
    peace
On their tossing boats in winter, when the storm-trumps never
    cease :

When the surges yearned to swallow man and boat within their
    graves
I had told them how the Saviour closed the wild mouths of the
    waves.

I had told them—and they listened, with stern faces very still—
That the raging deep was subject to a Father's loving will ;
That the maddest wave was free not from its halter and its chain,
Though it seemed to us unfettered as it coursed along the main.

I had said, while all around us streamed the cataracts of the
    foam,
" God is lord of the wild waters, and of all ye love at home ;
Here the waves' throats howl and raven, but on shore the storm
    is done,
And your children gather blossoms on the cliffs beneath the sun.

"There they pluck the golden trefoil, while our vessel sways and
    rocks,
With its brave bows never swerving at the rude waves' countless
    shocks :
There they gather the sea-poppies ; God is guarding every one ;
Here he rules in mist and darkness, there he smiles within the
    sun.

" Fathers, mothers, little children—he can shield you one and
    all ;
Aye, without his loving mandate not a sparrow's plume shall fall,
No white feather of a sea-bird, till the course of time is run :
God can lighten the sea's darkness, he is mightier than the sun."

I had comforted the widow, I had soothed the soul bereaved,
I had sought to bring God's comfort to the spirit as it grieved ;
I had preached the eternal rapture of the life beyond the grave
While in hearing of my hearers death's voice sobbed within the
          wave.

In the little whitewashed chapel, with its hideous walls and pews,
I had preached to eager hearers Christ's, the gospel's, great good
          news ;
I had preached of heavenly glories till the hearers' eyes grew dim,
Aye, and preached of hell's red terrors with insistence stern and
          grim.

I had said to the poor woman, when they brought her darling
          home
With his yellow hair still dripping with the clammy beads of
          foam,
" Christ has taken—yield him gently.   Still your sweetheart with
          him waits
Smiling, watching, tarrying for you, just behind the golden gates."

I had preached, and striven to comfort—now I knew it was a lie :
Of all hopeless hearts and weary the most hopeless heart was I,
The most hopeless and the weariest—I the preacher of the Lord,
I who trusted in his mercy, had been smitten by his sword.

I had preached of hell's red terrors—now my preaching all was
          done ;
'Tis not hard to preach of darkness in the full light of the sun :

Easy it is to tell hell's captives to break through their prison bars
When oneself is steering heavenward in the full light of the stars !

I had preached, but now I knew it, the eternity of pain ;
Heaven was lost, aye lost for ever, or there was no heaven to
    gain :
Now I knew what I had dreamed of, what the godless void may
    be—
Hell's fierce breakers stretching onward, and no Christ's foot on
    the sea.

Yes, my noblest dreams were scattered. I had dreamed that
    God had sent
Annie, my one love, my darling, my one priceless treasure lent
By the Lord to me, to lift me—so I fancied—yet more near
Ever unto him in spirit ; a delusion—that was clear.

I had planned a perfect marriage, but my thoughts too swiftly
    ran :
Bitter is it to discover that the goodness is in man,
Not in God as we were dreaming ; bitter is it to perceive,
That though evil horrifies us, God it does not wound nor grieve.

Bitter is it, passing bitter, when our purity outgrows
God's, and therefore courts defilement ; wretched is it when one
    knows
That a true man's dream of woman, loveliest dream that life
    affords,
Is a lonely dream for ever,—even his own and not the Lord's !

Oh my darling whom I worshipped, whom I would have died to
　win
In her pureness, her perfection, safe from weakness, stain, and
　sin ;
Whom my whole soul would have honoured, in her tender girlish
　bloom ;
Whom God gave me—for one moment—in a gaslit London
　room !

Was it noble, was it worthy of the Lord of heaven to make
Her my destined bride a harlot? was it godlike thus to take
From a weary heart its gladness, from a lonely soul its light,
When I lost her for a lifetime, having won her for a night?

Just one night—aye, one night only—and one night in such a
　place !
There to see her gazing at me with the same sweet girlish face
Little hardened, scarcely altered, that I used to watch at home
While the moon outside the window lit the pure wild wastes of
　foam.

She the same—yet not the same one—nevermore the same to
　me
Who had held my hand in silence by the blue clear Cornish sea ;
Who as pure as heaven above us had beheld the stars arise
Over sinless leagues of ocean, with love's starlight in her eyes.

She the very same for ever—with the wealth of raven hair,
Throat whose every curve was perfect, yes if anything more fair ;

Yet with something lost for ever—with one jewel on the track
Dropped—and never through all ages shall we win that jewel
   back !

She the same in sinful London—she, with girlish eyes and heart,
Now a sinner, yes a sinner—just a portion, just a part
Of the wanton selfish city, she who might have been my own ;
Now all London stood between us—we should never be alone !

I had preached of Christ's redemption.   Could his rich blood
   wash out this ?
Could he undo what had happened, and unfasten kiss from
   kiss ?
Could he link by link remove it, sin's once-fashioned deadly
   chain ?
Set before me my lost darling in her whiteness once again ?

Could he take the feeling from me—though I found her very
   fair—
That another hand before me had caressed the raven hair ?
That malignant haunting horror, of all poisonous pangs the worst,
That each touch had been discounted, that each kiss had been
   rehearsed !

Such a bridal—such a bride-bed—with the drama played before
And the author's step, it might be, even now close at the door :
Such a bride and such a marriage—just one hour love in the
   room,
Love's voice singing for one moment, then the silence of the
   tomb !

Singing—ah! and such a song too—not the song sung by the sea
When the envious throstle clamoured for the copyright from me :
When the gold sun paused to listen, though but half his toil was
　　done ;
When the sun forgot the cornfields, and the lark forgot the sun.

This was something like the cadence—still I carry it in my brain :
How the words light up those cornfields with the sun's old glory
　　again !
How the words, though sweet and simple, sum the history up in
　　brief,
For a covert threat lurks in them and a prophecy of grief !

The blue sea brings its greeting to the swallow,
　　Then drives it inland with the wild sea-storm.
The fields are crowned with bloom, but cold winds follow :
　　Hardly the flowers can keep each other warm.
The sun cries to the sky, " Soon must we part :
I love you—yes—but not with all my heart ! "

" We love you, yes, but with a love most fleeting,"
　　So cry the stars to the eternal night :
" Farewell ! farewell ! the sun awaits our greeting ;
　　We loved the darkness, now we love the light.
Farewell ! farewell ! the tenderest souls must part :
'Tis good to love—but not with all the heart."

" I love you ! " cries the vessel to the river :
　　" I love your ripples and their harmless glee ;

Yet one day with delicious shock and shiver
  My bows will meet the white waves of the sea.
I love you, river, yet we needs must part:
I love you well—but not with all my heart."

" I love you !" cries the sea's voice to the vessel,
  " But I have loved a thousand loves before
Then flung them, after one wild amorous wrestle,
  Pale and discarded on the loveless shore.
New loves await me, when the old loves depart:
My locks are grey, but youth is in my heart."

Then her ringing clear voice deepened though the song more
  cruel grew ;
Still I carry it in my memory, for the cadence thrilled me through :
Ah ! how well the song expressed her—all her soul through the
  refrain
Chimed out silver-sweet and girlish, yet so careless of man's pain.

" I love you, friend—I love you, strong and tender,
  And full of care for me and kindly thought:
I love the summer morning's golden splendour,
  The frosty lacework on our windows wrought:
And yet I love not wholly, only in part ;
All things I love—yet not with all my heart.

" There is a something still before me waiting ;
  I stand and tremble on the wave-washed shore:

I stand in doubt, uncertain, hesitating ;
  Love it may be has lovelier gifts in store.
Love only as yet has given himself in part :
Me Love has loved, but not with all his heart !

" If with your heart you love me, let the swallow
Point out the road to other shores than ours :
I am a bird of passage—I would follow
  The blue-winged birds to lands of gayer flowers.
They tarry not—they love us, yet depart ;
And I would follow them with all my heart.

" I love you well, but yet the hours are flying ;
  The summers pass us by—they gaze in scorn :
Yes, hour by hour the golden days are dying ;
  Life dies, while pleasure hardly yet is born.
Oh give your bright-winged bird leave to depart,
And I will love you then with all my heart !"

Where she found the song, I know not—nor if here and there a word
She had altered, lightly singing, like the light heart of a bird :
In some book maybe she found it ; he who wrote it knew not then
That on one heart 'twould be written with a dagger, not a pen.

*   *

I would leave the accursed city—I would take her child with me,
So she begged me, so she wished it—I would seek the old pure
  sea :
There by stainless wastes of water, by blue wavelets undefiled,
It might be a fairer future might await the sinless child.

It was something—just a little—for the lost sad mother's sake
That I still might do—a little—so my heart not quite might
     break ;
Break not yet at least,—my life's work not as yet was wholly done ;
I had yet to preach of darkness, I the prophet of the sun.

I had yet to preach the gospel of despair to all mankind :—
I had preached of Christ and gladness, but my spirit then was
     blind ;
I had yet to preach of darkness—yet to lift my voice on high,
Higher than all the waves proclaiming, "Christ's whole message
     is a lie."

How my thoughts flew back remembering how some fifteen years
     before
I had borne away the mother, then a child, and left the door
Of the hospital in London thanking God that I could give
To a dying woman comfort—then it seemed worth while to live !

Annie—little dark-eyed darling—how I proudly bore you away !
How I showed you to my mother ! how I watched you at your
     play !
How I bought you dolls and trinkets, and a hundred wondrous
     toys,
And tin soldiers—till my mother said that soldiers were for boys.

When the railway journey ended, the long journey to Penzance,
How I watched your bright eyes sparkle, when you saw the white
     waves dance :
How I thought, "There yet is sunlight, if all other sunlight dies ;
This is God's eternal sunlight—even the light in sinless eyes ! "

Oh, how well I can remember when the sea flashed on your sight
How you stretched your eyes wide open, with a laugh of pure
    delight ;
How with that same voice which, later, made the throstle's heart
    despond
With an eager gasp you asked me, " Are there ducks upon that
    pond ? "

How you loved to gather sea-weed—red and green and white and
    pink ;
I can see to-day your shudder—I can see your fingers shrink
At their sudden startling contact with that cold flower of the sea,
The bright scarlet turquoise-beaded furtive sea-anemone.

With what pride—I can remember—you once brought me in
    your hand
A translucent lovely treasure which the sea had tossed on land ;
Just a piece of broken bottle—but to us it seemed to be
Surely a priceless emerald stolen from the fairies of the sea !

Then the terror—oh ! the terror—when beneath that granite slab
Your poor finger came in contact, cruel contact, with a crab ;
How I kissed the poor pinched finger—how I soothed your sobs
    and sighs—
And we bore the rude crab homeward in a teacup for a prize.

Then the rapture, the wild rapture, when we saw the goby gleam
In our net at last, a captive—the fulfilment of a dream
That had lasted the whole summer, for that summer's dearest
    wish
Was to capture from his rock-pool that swift-darting tiny fish.

Then the glories of the shore too—there were butterflies on land,
Fair to see, but hard to capture. Once you brought me in your
    hand
(Now a hundred bright wing-cases count for nothing on your fan)
Such a prize—a great rose-beetle—splendid past the speech of
    man !

Has one jewel in London glittered with as fairy-like a gleam
As the spots upon the trout's side which we jerked from out the
    stream,
Making all the alder-bushes—and our clothes too—wringing
    wet,
With a happy sudden side-jerk of the diamond-dropping net?

Oh those were our golden moments, though more golden were
    to come
When I read you in the quiet and the silence of our home
Tales of giants, dwarfs, and ogres, tales of knights and ladies
    fair
—Thinking all the time "no lady ever had my Annie's hair!"

How you loved the marvellous stories—nothing as you older
    grew
Was too marvellous, too fantastic, too miraculous for you :
Yes—I sometimes even think that our old readings' very charm
Turned your mind from life's real duties, did your dawning spirit
    harm.

Take for instance that grand story which would move you even
    to tears
Of the wondrous Fairy Palace which no mortal footstep nears,
Magic Palace of the Seasons where the seasons four are one,
Where the white snow gleams for ever, yet it melts not at the sun.

How your fancy seized the notion of the mingled seasons there,
Of the scents of summer mixing with the snowflakes in the air,
Of the measureless bright Palace where eternal summer gleamed,
Where the nightingale for ever sang and loved, and loved and
    dreamed.

How you revelled in the notion of the fragrant summer room
Where for ever all the roses of the fay-land were in bloom :
Where the leafage of a summer that no mortal might behold
Lit the deep trees with a splendour mortal tongue has never told.

Summer—yes, eternal summer—in that fragrant central room
Nought of darkness, nought of horror, nought of sorrow, nought
    of gloom :
That is how your life, my darling (so I murmured !) ought to be ;
Perfect happiness proceeding from unsullied purity.

But the Palace—the bright Palace—oh ! my fancy lingers there ;
If a mortal could but find it, and could breathe its sinless air—
If again we could but find it, how contented we should be
Even its solemn winter chamber, not the summer room, to see !

For within the winter chamber endless hoary winter reigned ;
Whitest snows of earthly mountains would seem muddy, blurred
    and stained,

By the pure unsullied whiteness of the eternal snows within
That far-off enchanted Palace, where no heart had dreamed of
    sin.

Yes, the keen eyes of the fairies might with reason view with
    scorn
Even the bluest ice that glitters on our lordly Matterhorn :
Not from noblest Alpine summit was there ever view so grand
As from even the humblest summit of the hills of fairy-land.

And the night, the wondrous night there, when upon the peaks
    sublime
Fell a silence, such a silence ; on the shadowy hills of time
That our Wordsworth made immortal, when the moon breathed
    down her spell
And the stars shed forth their glamour, never such a silence fell :

Silence perfect, strange, unearthly—silence as of utmost peace—
Such as when the trumpet clamours of the warring wild winds
    cease
On a sudden in mid-ocean, and the sea with gentle lips
Whispers, " I was only playing," to the sea-birds and the ships :

Silent peace—I used to fancy—such as Jesus might have known
When he murmured " It is finished," when he stood at last
    alone
Face to face with labour ended ; peace no mortal sorrow mars :
Such the calm was when those ice-peaks glittered underneath the
    stars !

Sinless calm and peace most holy, so the dear old fable ran,
Brooded o'er those stainless summits never soiled by foot of
    man :
Calm divine and rapture perfect—through the crags no thunder
    rolled ;
There the sun rose storm-defiant, there he sank in cloudless gold.

That was far too grand for mortals—we could breathe with easier
    breath
In that Palace of the Seasons where life mocks the sword of
    death
When we entered the bright chamber where rich autumn reigned
    superb,
Crowned with fiery leaves and sunshine, and with glowing corn
    and herb.

(That was just what took your fancy—to have all good gifts in
    one—
Noble whiteness of the winter, nobler glory of the sun ;
Spring's soft colours never dreading, with a pang of sudden grief,
Death that turns the green leaf living to the golden dying leaf.)

For within the fairy palace the rich woods of autumn shone,
Forest after forest flaming into distances unknown :
No such colours in the far-famed Indian summer of the West
Ever burned on leafy banners, ever flashed from leafy crest.

Fairy oaks and fairy beeches, scarlet maples, glittered there,
And such radiance gleamed along them from the magic heights
    of air

That, had mortal vision seen them, mortal tongue could never
    tell
How the tossing waves of colour on the light wind rose and fell.

Even here was contradiction.   What would fairy landscapes be
Without wizard feats of colour, glorious incongruity?
There were roses, there were snow-drifts, there were yellow
    autumn leaves—
There were dahlias by the ice-ponds, there was frost upon the
    sheaves.

But the loveliest of the chambers in the Palace was the one
Where the green leaves gave a softness to the full flame of the
    sun :
Where the may-bloom ever glistened, but more fragrant far than
    ours ;
Where the children of the fairies gathered never-dying flowers.

There was spring-time everlasting—not a spring that fades away
Leaving littered in the foot-paths trodden blossoms of the may,
Not a spring that shrinks from summer, but a spring that still
    will last
When the earthly flowers and foliage of a million springs are
    past.

You with sunlight in your glances, and with spring-time in your
    heart,
Seemed yet fuller fairer meaning to the story to impart :
When the fairy queen came singing through her palace, every
    word
Seemed to suit you, to express you—it was Annie that I heard.

Ours is the unfading pleasure
That never can grow old ;
A joy beyond man's measure,
Delight no tongue has told.
No death within our palace
For ever will there be,—
No wild storm's wrath or malice,
No terror of the sea.

If man with all his sorrow
Could reach us where we dwell
There would be no to-morrow
For fairy mount or fell :
If man with all his sadness
Within our gates could stand
There would be no more gladness
Then left for fairy-land.

For man would bring his yearning,
His hopes and fears and sighs,
His passions fierce and burning,
His feverish enterprise :—
We post our keen-eyed warders
Along the frontier line ;
Upon the magic borders
Their fairy sabres shine.

If man could ever enter
The fairy-land, what grief
Would thrill its very centre,
A horror past belief !

For all our flowers are stainless
  And all our fields are fair :
The life we live is painless,
  But man's life means despair.

Never the fairy warders
  Will let one mortal pass :
Imperative their orders—
  Were they to yield alas !
What thunderous change of weather
  Upon our hills would loom,
For man and sin together
  Would bring about our doom.

But man with heart infernal
  Will never trespass here ;
His sentence is eternal,
  His destiny is clear :
He sees the golden portal
  Through silent slumber gleam,—
He cries " I am immortal !"
  He wakes—It is a dream.

❊   ❊

I was dreaming of the Palace—I was in the railway train
Bearing Annie, ever Annie, to the old lost home again :
I was dreaming of the fairies, but my fairy queen was gone ;
I was only alas ! a mortal, broken-hearted and alone.

No, the pure-eyed child was with me, with her hand within my
  hand,
Just a stray gold blossom-petal drifted here from fairy-land !
But the mother, my lost fairy—she would never, nevermore,
See the fairy legions mustering all along the mystic shore !

She would never hear the bugles of the fairy squadrons sound,
See the fairies line the frontier, guard the old enchanted ground :
She would never see the gateways at her coming open wide
And the fairy guards saluting, straight, erect, on either side.

Day by day the guards would wonder that her chariot never rolled,
Drawn by milk-white noble prancers, through the glittering gates
  of gold :
Day by day the keen-eyed watchers, peering out, would peer in
  vain ;
Never trumpet in the distance ! never dust upon the plain !

There the guards will wait for ever—there the sentinels will stand—
All will still go on for ever as of old in fairy-land :
As of old, with one thing wanting—not at evening nor at morn
Through the gates with shouts of triumph will the fairy queen be
  borne.

Though the fairy soldiers know not, though the sinless peaks of
  snow
In the wondrous winter chamber smiling on the meads below,
Though these know not, I could tell them where their mourned-
  for mistress dwells—
In a land remote for ever from their stormless fields and fells.

—Yes, despair and death have triumphed—that is what I have
    to preach :
Christ is slain and Satan victor—that is what I have to teach :
For the fairy queen I worshipped in the London smoke-stained
    air
Keeps her court now, and the basest gains at once admittance
    there.

Now the meanest bring credentials.   Have they money in their
    hand ?
Then they gain a ready entrance into London's fairy-land.
The old questions are not asked now—it is not as it has been—
Now the only question asked is, " Have they presents for the
    queen ? "

        *   *

Well the years sped on in Cornwall, but I'll pass those swift years
    by ;
Nothing varied the vast calmness of the expanse of sea and sky.
All the love in me was softened into fatherhood again :
Ah, the love in man enables Fate to inflict the endless pain !

All went on in steady sequence—that is how the days depart
When Fate lurks behind the sunshine with new dark deeds in his
    heart :
Just the same they seem to pass us, smiling, sun-kissed, every
    one ;
But Fate, black-browed, thunder-wielding, stands alert behind the
    sun.

K

—So in summer when the ocean with its soft voice to the land
Sings its love-song, sings so gently, he whose heart can under-
stand,
Versed in all the ways of Nature, still within the sound can hear
Something of its wintry storm-voice, when its wild wrath stuns
the ear.

For the one same sea in summer to the listening sunlit shore
Says with voice as of a lover, " Lo, I love you, I adore ! "
And in winter to the cliff-sides, ribbed with granite though they
be,
" Lo, I hate you—ye shall perish from the pathway of the sea ! "

Fate arose at last : a letter in the old handwriting came—
How the light of coming evil flashed across my eyes like flame !
Half I broke it open—waited—tore the envelope once more—
Trembled then again and waited—till I read it on the shore.

She was dying, said the letter, dying in London all alone—
Would I come once more and see her ? (Would a mother leave
her own ?)
So once more I journeyed townward, took the route I knew so
well ;
Left the quiet sea behind me, entered London—entered hell.

Not the same as when I left it was the once well-furnished room :
All to-day was desolation, all was emptiness and gloom.
No silk curtains to the bed-posts, not a picture now was there ;
Just a bed—a dying woman—a white ghost with raven hair !

Yes, the fairy guards were waiting, far away in fairy-land,
But the fairy queen lay dying in a bed-room off the Strand.
Not again in fairy regions would her golden sceptre wave :
She was just a poor lost woman, five days' journey from her
    grave !

He had left her in man's fashion, wearied when the prize was
    gained :
Of the wedding-robes of passion not a worn-out shred remained !
—Left her all alone in London, with the one vile bitter word
" Earn your living, you are young yet ; " was there any Christ
    who heard ?

Was there any Christ, I wonder, who had seen the whole thing
    done,
Seen the girl's heart grow to woman's, seen the woman lightly
    won,
Watched at night within the bed-room, seen the man come, then
    depart,
Any Christ—we'll grant his godhead—but with manhood in his
    heart ?

Was there any Christ who knew it, all the lies the man had
    told,
All the lying talk of marriage—who had seen the ring of gold,
Just the saddest of all tokens, worn to shirk the social ban,
Worn to link her to her sisters, not to link her to the man ?

Was there any Christ who knew it and whose pure true heart
    contained
All a strong man's mightiest passion, all a strong God's anger
    chained ?
Any Christ whose deep love blended in its vast and complex
    whole
All the pity in man's deep nature, all the love in woman's soul ?

Was there any Christ who knew it ? was he silent in the sky ?
Did he come on earth to trifle, just to love a few and die ?
Did he idle at Capernaum ? Did he jest in Galilee ?
Was he wearied with the blood-sweat ? Did he faint on Calvary ?

Was his pity quite exhausted ? Was his healing power outworn ?
Did he wear just for one season one ephemeral crown of thorn ?
In Jerusalem he triumphed ? When he rose from out the grave
Did he deem his work was over, that no souls were left to save ?

Did he deem when man betrayed him that no Judas would arise
In the ages that he saw not, under Western sunless skies ?
Did his soul foresee the horror that the years to come would
    bring ?
Was he only for one moment just a pale apparent King ?

Was his kingship wholly vested in the moments that he spent
Here on earth with men and women, ere the Temple's veil was
    rent ?
Could he face the sin of London ? Could he see our streets by
    night
Yet retain his stormless splendour, and his crown's imperial light ?

Could he bear to see our city—could he know the evil done
Every hour, yes every moment, when the gaslights drown the sun?
Every night some woman ruined, every night some base seeds
  sown
For whose harvests of fierce evil not God's whole blood could
  atone !

Had he seen *this* woman ruined?   Had he followed Annie's life?
Would he not now track the villain, hunt him down with dagger
  or knife ?
Would he not proclaim God's justice—if a God indeed there be—
God's eternal hate of evil, God's unsullied majesty ?

—So the thoughts in swift wild sequence flew with frenzy through
  my brain
As I saw the dying woman, heard her speak yet once again,
Heard her tell with broken accents all her story of despair ;
Then my whole soul cried out Godward as I watched her lying
  there,

Cried out heavenward : " If the mountains or the lurid storm-
  clouds hold
Any strong God, a Jehovah, as the peoples deemed of old,
If there be a God of anger, past the anger of the sea,
And behind the love of Jesus, noble wrath's intensity ;

" If there be within the thunder still a living God more strong,
If the lightning's sword be *his* sword, if his soul detests the
  wrong,
If the righteous power of judgment yet within some God remains,
If he be not blind for ever, if his sceptre he retains ;

"If he be not weak or slothful, be not sunk in lethargy,
Let him mark this London death-bed, let him gaze from heaven
    and see:
Let him stay no longer dallying with his minor toils on high,
Let him stoop to us in London, let him quit the starry sky;

"Let him rise up in his anger—as they say of old he rose—
Let his sword leap from the scabbard, on the hilt his fingers
    close;
Let him carry out my curse now, carry it out by day, by night,
Let the living God do justice, let the Lord God hear and smite;

"Let the living God do justice, let the living God proclaim
Once again his deathless glory, and the greatness of his name;
Let him follow with his vengeance this one man, where'er he be—
Let my soul's curse light upon him, let it traverse land and sea;

"If he scale the lofty mountains, let my curse, God, still be
    there;
Let it peal within the thunder, let it sound through sunlit air;
Let it follow him all his lifetime, let it ring his earthly knell,
Let it follow him to the graveyard, let it haunt his steps in hell.

"Follow thou, Lord, with thy curse too—as if there were only one,
As if he alone were living, he alone beneath the sun:
Follow thou with thy strong curse too—if thou lettest him go free,
Then may one man's curse for ever light, thou recreant God,
    on thee!"

           *   *

Then my whole soul changed to pity. Now the storm of wrath
    was dead :
Very tenderly I raised her, and I kissed the raven head,
Kissed it gently, oh so gently—and I kissed the pale sad brow,
Thinking, "Though past words I loved her, yet I never loved till
    now ! "

All the fieriest early passion had not half the strength or power
Of the sense of deathless pity that transfused my soul that hour ;
I was conscious now of nothing save a love so deep, so strong,
That the sense of horror vanished, and the deadly sense of wrong.

Here was death to make atonement for the vast wrong done to
    me :
Here was sin's whole end, commencement of a pure eternity.
Sin had done its violent utmost to degrade and to defile ;
Life had strangled her young laughter—death had given her back
    her smile.

Yes, her smile—for as she lay there such a sweetness through her
    eyes
Came with lovely radiance gleaming as through stormiest sunset
    skies
When an autumn wild day closes and the sullen vapours part
And we know the sun is living and that love lives at his heart.

Just the very same old sweetness, only sweeter so it seemed,
That I worshipped when that sunset on the far-off cliff-sides
    gleamed—
When she gave the waves their laughter, gave its lustre to the sky,
Gave the evening star its splendour, even her girlish purity.

Then I thought, " Whatever happens in the land to which she
    goes,
Whether life or love be waiting, or profound and sweet repose,
One thing surely is not waiting, surely it is not in God's plan
When the grave's past to confront her with the lies and lust of
    man.

" Whether angels group around her, or the friends of former years,
Some with outstretched hands of welcome, some with grave eyes
    full of tears,
Whether Jesus there be waiting, this at least I know right well,
That the villain who betrayed her will be leagues away in hell.

" God will turn hell's keys upon him, God will keep him safe
    within
The dark region he exults in, even the land of lust and sin :
If in God's heart or in Christ's heart any noble anger be
The destroyer is damned for ever, but the victim shall go free ! "

             *   *

Then she signed to me to listen, and I stooped above the bed :
" I know better now, forgive me," with the same sweet voice she
    said,
Yes the same, but sadly weak now, that had won my heart of old ;
Then she grasped my hand so firmly in a tight strange childlike
    hold—

" Guard my darling, guard my daughter, save her from this world
    of sin ;
There's another Annie left you, there's a victory left to win :

If you see her heart misguided, if you see her going wrong,
Kill her . . . kill her—that way save her—you can save, if
   you are strong.

" If you see her copy her mother, if you see her growing too like,
Be more merciful than God is, call on pure-souled death to
   strike !
Swear to me, whatever happens, you will never let her be
Any rich man's sport and plaything, never let her grow like me.

" Do not speak to her of her mother—or, if you must speak at all,
Only speak of early days, dear, long before the mother's fall :
If she wants to know my ending, asks you what became of me,
Say my death was strange and lonely . . . say that I was
   drowned at sea. . . .

" Don't forget me, for I loved you—though I did not know it
   then—
You were grave and I light-hearted, and I could not fathom men :
When they told me that they loved me, I believed it, till I knew
That the grave love was the true love—till at last I fathomed
   you.

" Till at last I understood, dear, wholly learned and not in part
How my folly had made you suffer, how my sin had wrecked
   your heart :
Yes, at last I understood you, but the knowledge came in vain ;
Now it could not bring atonement—it could only deepen pain.

" Why, I wonder, is it—always—that a woman's soul must win
Perfect knowledge of what love is through the trial first of sin ?
Perfect knowledge of the noblest through experience of the
    worst ?
When she's on the road to Jesus, why must Judas win her first ?

" Ah ! I cannot understand it—nothing now to me is clear
Save this one thing, that I love you and I like to feel you near :
Come yet closer, come quite close now, for I cannot see you
    well ;
Tell me, is God very angry ? will he send my soul to hell ?

" I don't fear him—I can face him, if there's love within his mind ;
If he loves me as you love me, he will never be unkind :
If he loves me as you love me, I could love him in the end ;
And the next world seems so lonely—I want some one for a
    friend !

" Shall I have to be alone there ?   I was frightened long ago
In that dark strange cave in Cornwall—when I went alone, you
    know,
Seeking ferns within the cavern.   When you found me, all was
    right,
For the sunshine came in with you, and that gloomy cave
    grew bright.

" Put your hand beneath the pillow—I have still some sea-weed
    there,
Dried, in that small sealed-up packet, and a tuft of maiden-hair

That we gathered—you've forgotten?—in remembrance of the
cave
And my grand deliverance from it : I should like them in my
grave.

" They may serve there to remind me—who can tell us? —it may
be—
That you saved me from that darkness and the hoarse threats of
the sea :
They may serve to give me hope there "—then the voice failed
—then she said,
" It is dark again, dear—kiss me . . . " as I kissed her she
was dead.

*   *

Soon I passed into the darkness of the quiet street outside,
Just to seek the last sad tendance for a woman who had died ;
That was all in outward seeming—just to send a human frame
Living help in its last journey to the dust from whence it came.

That was all in outward seeming : as I turned into the Strand
What a rage and crush of people, what a crowd on either hand!
Life was hurrying on for ever in its immemorial stream ;
Which was truth, my whole soul wondered—which, I wondered,
was the dream ?

Which was life in very truth now, which was after all most
sweet ?
Were they living, these lost women, as they pressed along the
street,

Coarse, with coarser men companions—were they living, or was
  she
Rather living ?   Had the dead soul won life's genuine victory ?

As I gazed into the faces, rouged and pencilled, sad and worn,
Through my whole soul surged a torrent of immense tempes-
  tuous scorn :
" Surely God's defeat is patent, his indelible disgrace
Writ at large, for all men's reading, in each lost girl's eyes and
  face !

" These have perished, with no shepherd.   What has Jesus done
  to save
These poor English girls and women from a deeper deadlier
  grave
Than the grave wherein they laid him ?   Once he suffered,
  then 'twas o'er ;
Woman's pain had no beginning : it will last for evermore.

" Where is right and where is justice ?   All is accident and
  chance.
As I passed just now that woman I saw deep within her glance
All the latent power of loving that in happier sisters leads
Their own souls to heights of virtue, those they love to noble
  deeds.

" Must one woman be degraded, while another woman soars
Clad in rustling silks and satin towards the heavenly golden
  doors ?

Why must all the stars, obsequient, lend one honeymoon their
light
While another woman in darkness changes husbands every
night?

"Why must one display with rapture, happy, wifely, pure and
sweet,
All her gifts and wedding presents, with the whole world at her
feet,
While another, just as noble, had her life's chance been the
same,
Dips her soul each night more deeply in the nameless mire of
shame?

"Why must one parade in Venice, with her husband by her side,
While another walks in London, all the town's promiscuous
bride?
Analyse them when they started, eyes and lips and mind and
heart —
It may be you'd hardly have known them, after all, at first,
apart?

"Why must one child in the cradle by a mother rocked to sleep
Rest, while through the foggy darkness other weary footsteps
creep,—
Weary footsteps of some mother, in her madness carrying down
Her first baby to the river, for the cradling waves to drown?"

*   *

So I thought, and through my spirit a wild sense of godship ran,
But a godship fierce, nefarious, not a godship good for man.

I had grown in strength of being, but my faith in God was
    gone :
I was standing silent, self-poised—loving truth and that alone.

As I watched the crowded pavement and the sad lost faces
    there
All my soul was rent and tortured by a measureless despair ;
Yet a living force within me seemed to meet the sense of
    wrong,
Living, holy, deathless, godlike, inextinguishably strong :

" Though God's sinning last for ever, and man's suffering "—so I
    cried—
" Though in vain the sad world's lover on the cross, it may be,
    died,
Still the spirit of love within me shall not falter, shall not pass,—
I will preach the only gospel that is left to preach alas !

" I have preached it down in Cornwall, I will preach it here in
    town,
Take the faded wreath from Jesus, and bestow the future's
    crown
On the thinker, Schopenhauer—him whose heart discerned the
    first
That man's truest highest duty is to face the very worst.

" Just to know the worst that can be, and to face it as he can,
That is man's last highest duty, just the last hope left for man :
Just to know that all is over, that the life he deemed so fair
Born in darkness, ends in darkness, born in chaos, closeth
    there.

" Just to know that all is mockery—that the one mistake man
   made
Was to travel into sunlight from the unconscious realms of
   shade;
That the one thing left to achieve now is again to travel back
Towards the unconscious realm we came from, leaving no sign on
   the track :

" Dropping not one single blossom on the road by which we
   came
Back to realms of peace unconscious from the conscious realm
   of shame ;
Leaving nought to tell creation that the monstrous thing was
   done,
Not a plank upon the waters, not a tower beneath the sun.

" This I'll preach, the newer gospel, preach it stronglier than
   before,
Preach it in the towns and cities, on the mountains, on the
   shore :
I will tell poor sad lost women, 'There is peace within the
   grave;
Lo! the river is your lover—there is rest within its wave.

" ' When God built up cruel London, when he changed it into
   hell,
In one point the Lord had mercy for he set the Thames as
   well
Ever flowing through the city, and its voice will never cease
To proclaim to life's pale victims, " 'Neath my waters there is
   peace ! "

" ' With a tenderer voice than Jesus now the river's waves proclaim
To each man by anguish maddened, to each woman lost in
shame,
" Come to me all ye that labour, each with heavy-laden breast ;
Plunge within my waves and trust me—I will give your spirits
rest.

" ' " I will give you rest eternal—not the rest of heaven, for there
There would be a new beginning, even the birth of new despair;
I will give you rest unending, even the rest of sunless gloom,
Peace from pain and calm immortal, and the silence of the
tomb.

" ' " Close beside my starlit margin still the wheels of life shall
roll
But your spirits shall be mingled with my dim unconscious
soul :
What a gulf between the living in the gaslit streets hard by
And the souls who have the courage just to conquer life and
die !

" ' " God and man have had no mercy ?   I am loving more than
they.
Lo ! the stream of life goes pouring past my margin day by day,
Down the Strand and through the City.   Does it ever reach a
goal ?
Does it ever with its current lift to peace one single soul ?

" ' " Never!   But my waters gather every human stray and waif,
Very tenderly they hold them and they clasp them close and
    safe.
I am gentler than the life-stream : what I gather to my breast
That I part not with for ever, but I bear it down to rest.

" ' " I the lover universal give no common gifts indeed,
In my eyes the lily's worthless, and the rose is but a weed ;
But my passion is unfailing—each who seeks me I embrace,
And I lift the gold hair clinging round the drowned white neck
    and face :

" ' " Softly, tenderly, I lift it—and I kiss the quiet eyes ;
Dead are all the old thoughts within them, tears of grief will never
    rise :—
Then the next night I am ready, for despair life's active slave
On the next night brings, it may be, some new victim to my
    wave.

" ' " Never harem had such treasures as my silent waves contain
For what life has but half ruined they receive without disdain :
Though the heart of God grow weary, though God's voice
    grow hoarse with scorn,
In my heart is endless pity for each being cursed and born.

" ' " Final peace on all who trust me, that my waters can bestow :
Ask the moon who watches nightly, ask the stars that come
    and go
Through the ink-dark heavens above me ; though man's every
    joy must flee
Rest my waters still can furnish, as they find it in the sea." '

L

" Ah ! the sea—I'll tell the sailors not to dread the angry deep,
For its wrath is but a semblance, in its depths is griefless sleep:
I will preach that if true mercy had by Jesus' heart been shown
He had let the wild waves swallow that frail boat that held his
     own.

" ' Death is peace and life is anguish ; death's the end, the perfect
     goal ; '
This I'll preach in tones of triumph to each listening suffering
     soul :
I shall win, maybe, more hearers — talk of joy, you seem to
     jest !—
But all mortal souls have suffered, and all sufferers long for
     rest.

" 'Other souls have loved before you, they have suffered, they
     have passed :
Now they call you from the sea-waves, now they summon from
     the blast.
Through a thousand storms they wrestled, through all stormy
     days but one—
That day bore them, wild with rapture, down to darkness from
     the sun.

" ' And our hope is just to join them, those old ancestors of ours,
Stalwart ghosts of brave old Vikings in the deep sea's crystal
     bowers ;
There they wait, the staunch old Norsemen—we shall join them,
     we shall be
Welcomed with a shout of triumph through the gateways of the
     sea.

" 'Though a million ships have safely sailed along the ocean way
Little heeded by the waters, not caressed of wind or spray,
Yet a chance is left for each one, for the ocean's heart is large ;
" Still it loves you " the wind whispers, as it sings along its
marge.

" 'Still the mighty ocean loves you—yes, the ocean's heart is
grand.
Has life failed to apprehend you ?   Still the sea can understand.
Are you weary of the pleasures and the loves of every day ?
There's a kiss fatigueless waiting on the white lips of the spray !

" ' Not in quiet gardens lighted by the soft light of the sun,
Nor in heavenly golden palace, shall your final bliss be won ;
Nay, beneath a stormier moonlight than the light that filled the
sky
When the sea to the Armada spake one sweet wild hoarse word :
" Die ! "

" 'Sweet and wild and hoarse and loving—life was waiting them
in Spain,
Life with all its feeble pleasures, its vast loss, its little gain ;
Then the infinite sea had mercy — while it baulked the
Spaniards' plan,
To its bosom's cold pure sweetness it clasped every vessel and
man.

" ' And for you too peace is waiting, even a sombre peace and
still :
Though your wives shall gaze out seaward from green headland
or from hill,

Though your sweethearts may be waiting, though your gardens
    all in bloom
May be waiting, yet a stronger is in waiting, even the tomb.

" 'Fairer, sweeter shall ye find it—where your fathers died of
    old
With the tossing waves around them, even the waters wide and
    cold,
Ye shall perish. Ye shall know not, wrapt for ever in sunless
    dreams,
Whether August roses redden, whether gold October gleams.'

"Thus I'll preach and they shall hear me, for despair is ever
    heard :
When the words of hope fall fruitless, every wingless barren
    word,
Then the human heart is gladdened, when along the icy air
Fly truth's deadly keenest arrows and the snow-shafts of despair."

          *   *

So I preached awhile in London, and I found that I could win
Hearers—not perhaps save sinners from the ways of wrath and
    sin
As I once (I thought) could save them : now I saved them by
    the cry
"Life is failure, life is torture—lay firm hold on death, and
    die ! "

Yes, I found I reached the people : they were ripe and ready
    there
In dark cruel evil London for the gospel of despair.

Many sufferers crowded round me, and I gave them of my best ;
Even the hope of rest from suffering, deep unconscious painless
    rest.

But I wearied of the city, and I longed to hear once more
The old angry white waves beating on the stedfast Cornish
    shore ;
Longed to see how time was dealing with the bright-eyed girl to
    whom
Life was still a fairy palace, not a dungeon or a tomb.

So I came, and when I saw her lo ! the budding rose had
    blown ;
While I toiled and preached in London, the swift sunny days
    had flown
Down in Cornwall : very lovely was the Annie whom I saw—
Yet a thrill of pain ran through me, and I watched her half in
    awe.

She had grown so like her mother ! all the past came storming
    back ;
Far away my mind went roaming on the old sad trodden track :
I was busy while in London—here my mind was void and free,
Open to the wind's weird whisper, and the wild voice of the
    sea.

So it came to pass that often, wandering on the cliffs apart,
Silent, nursing the grim memory of a vast pain in my heart,
Somewhat thus I dreamed and pondered : " Can it be that
    what we scan
Here on earth and call it evil, is but evil unto man ?

" In the sight of God all evil is but relative, no doubt ;
We behold it from within us, but he sees it from without ;
What is horrible past telling unto mankind, foul and grim,
Is the passing of a storm-cloud o'er blue waters unto him !

" True the woman as I saw her was a maiden with pure eyes,
Clean of heart and clean of fancy — but the Lord judged other-
        wise.
I considered her an angel, but God knew the girl was light,
Deemed her cut out for a mistress and a plaything : God was
        right.

" Every dream of hers was tender, pure and lovely, so I thought ;
But the Lord God—he was wiser — understood what he had
        wrought.
While I thought she was a seraph, far too fair for man to win,
God beheld the white wings draggle, dipped in filthy mire of sin.

" Which is wisest, which is truest ? Is the sight of God, or ours,
Keenest, swiftest, strongest, think you? While we dream of
        girls as flowers
White and soft and sweet and gracious, God with sight more
        piercing far
Sees them not as man conceives them : he beholds them as
        they are.

" He beholds the truth in all things, sees the alternate sides of
        life,
Sets one joy against another. Though Uriah lost his wife,

David won a royal pleasure : what to Christ, and Christ's, was
 loss
Was a triumph to the Jew-crowd, as they jested round the
 cross.

" Oh the misery to see it, oh the anguish to discern
How each joy upon some sorrow must for ever hinge and turn!
Nothing absolute, nought settled — from the murderer's point of
 view
Murder, doubtless, seems quite different, quite a saintly thing to
 do.

*   *

" Not a thought of me and Cornwall when she drained the cup
 of sin !
Yet it may be that was God's view—just to let the base man win.
Surely each man needs his pleasure ; what if one be low and
 base ?
Let him none the less (God says it?) kiss a pure girl's form
 and face.

" All is mixed and all is balanced : while the pale wife dreams at
 home
(As I dreamed of Annie, watching the blue waters and white
 foam)
He, her husband, revels doubtless, while he clean forgets her
 charms,
In a stronger pleasure, nestling in warm fervent younger arms.

"Does it matter? Can it matter?   When God totals the
    amount,
Ticks off item against item, can so small an item count?
No : or if the item matters, surely balanced it may be
By the pleasure soon accruing from the wife's adultery!

"Even the dream of good has left me—nought is right and
    nought is wrong,
For one Being carved the shrike's beak and composed the
    throstle's song ;
Made the sailor and his sweetheart — made the shark who in
    the sea
Just outside the harbour waiting says, 'Reserve one kiss for
    me.'

"God, no doubt, is very equal, grandly just, can sympathize
With the greed of gain that mixes with the vice in wanton eyes:
He who sends the wife her first-born, points the arrow of
    disease
That will slay the firstling shortly, smitten on the mother's
    knees.

"With the work-girl in her garret, with the queen on dainty bed,
With the viper lurking hidden 'neath the faggots in the shed,
With the vast plumes of the eagle, with the firefly's glowing
    wings,
With the lion as it couches, with the tiger as it springs—

"God has doubtless fellow-feeling, that in fine I must conclude,
With all these his various creatures, with each nestling in his
    brood :

Is the hand of any blood-stained? Yet, perhaps, the colour
 came
From the grip of God his Father, for his hand is dyed the
 same !

" When the man seduced my darling, was he copyist of the
 Lord ?
Would my blade have slain the Father, had I slain him with my
 sword ?
Is the lust we call so evil just an agent God employs
On the earth to further progress? Has the deadliest sin its
 joys ?

" Has the jaguar its keen rapture as its dripping sharp teeth tear?
And did God design the rapture, when he set the keen teeth
 there ?
Has the shark who rends the sailor, as he colours red the sea,
Some fierce wild orgasmic rapture, some predestined ecstasy ?

" Has the knave who trims the gibbet some delight in handling
 there
With his rough coarse cunning fingers the doomed neck he
 loves to bare ?
Is there something of a rapture, not all undivine, to him
In the vision of the gallows, and the scaffold black and grim ?

" When my darling to the scaffold where her pure sweet life was
 slain
Was conducted by a villain, did God will the cur should gain

Priceless knowledge, novel rapture ?   Was the thrill the villain
    knew
After all what he was made for ?   Does God crown the sinner
    too ?

"When I ignorant, unsuspecting, watched the maiden white
    moon rise
Was he at that very moment watching tears in Annie's eyes ?
Tears of virgin sweetness yielding, tears which I shall never see
Though I seek them through the pearl-fields of God's vast
    eternity.

" And was this the very thing then that God fully did intend ?
Was he working for the base man, was he just the villain's
    Friend ?
Was the rapture of the villain fore-ordained, and my despair,
By the God who made the fingers that let down my darling's
    hair ?

" Yes : God made the villain's fingers, joint by joint and bone by
    bone,
Made the lewd hands that caressed her and the voice that said
    ' My own !'
Made the base heart that betrayed her, made the lips that
    kissed and clung,
Set the blackness in the base heart, set the lies upon the
    tongue.

"And the worst is, does God count it just as righteous to
bestow
Such a gift on such a being as to let the worthier know
Through the pureness of a woman what of peace the world can
bring?
Is this justice of a true judge? Is this greatness of a king?"

*   *

Pureness! Yet what pureness ever in this dark world can there be?
Sweetest dream and yet the falsest is the dream of purity!
Even if your true love meet you with soft lips untouched by man
She has woman's past behind her, all the years since love began.

Is there one pure maid, one virgin, in this universe at all?
Did not all fair women totter at the first fair woman's fall?
— Pure she seems and very tender on the sacred nuptial night,
Yet in ages past with passion the same eyes, maybe, waxed
bright.

Is there one sure sign to show you that she has not lived before,
Watched the sunlit blue waves rippling on some quiet Eastern
shore?
Here i' the North to-day she loves you. Yet her eyes, it may
be, gleamed
Ages since with Southern passion, as in ancient Rome she
dreamed.

Your fair bride, maybe, was harlot in some Babylonian street:
Many ages she has traversed, and her lips were always sweet

And her laugh was always tender—she was dark-eyed, even the
    same,
When the towers of Carthage reddened into violent spires of
    flame.

You to-day may deem you hold her.   Not one soul is ever held
Safe, securely, by another!   By love's laws we are compelled
On from passion unto passion, on from wild hope to despair :
Maybe through a thousand ages she will still be here and fair.

Virgin !—let the weak dream perish, for God laughs the dream
    to scorn.
Is one life of any moment, is it of value to be born
Pure just for one single lifetime?   Every woman pure to-day
In some past life has been wanton, and has flung her soul away.

              *   *

Flung her soul away—as Annie now will fling away her soul,
For I see the horror coming, past a man's or God's control ;
Clearly I feel the horror coming—in her beauty and her pride
She will pass into the darkness, like her mother, my lost bride.

Surely soon her fate will seize her, for last week I saw her play
With a diamond on her finger—when I tore the ring away
Such a fierceness flashed upon me from her eyes that it was
    plain
Here was just the mother's nature, reproduced on earth again.

Reproduced—for good or evil?   Could I doubt which when
    she said,
" I would sell my soul for diamonds "—(how I thought of some
    one dead !
How a desolate room in London flashed upon my sight once
    more !
How I seemed to see men carry a black coffin from the door !)

Lovely is she, very lovely, and the donor of the ring
Doubtless covets her young beauty, full of sweetness as of spring :
Doubtless, eager to possess her, he who gave the child the toy
Will proceed—in man's sure manner—first to flatter, then destroy.

All the horror will return then.   Must I live to see her sink
Down hell's fiery seething centre, after gathering on the brink
Tender blossoms many-scented, flowers she finds exceeding fair ?
Must the old mad pain redouble and the speechless old despair ?

Doubtless all her heart is changing—as her mother's changed
    before ;
Now she hears no simple music in the waves' beat on the shore :
Now her longing when she watches the moon soar across the sky
Is the longing to escape us, and to revel in liberty !

Doubtless she too dreams of passion, when we think she dreams
    of prayer :
When her form is in the chapel, her swift spirit is not there ;
It is far away with some one—who can hold her or retain ?
God can chain the winged wild ocean, but a girl he cannot
    chain.

Neither man nor God can chain her, nor can strong life hold her
    fast :
Only death can ever hold her, when life's efforts all are past.
When life fails and when the Lord fails, man and death may
    sometimes win ;
When the sun fails, then the darkness puts an end to love and
    sin.

The eternal darkness closes, and the woman no more sees
Silvery moonlight on the waters, golden sunlight on the trees :
The eternal darkness saves her, whom nor God nor man could
    save.
Was she wanton on the green earth ? She is chaste within the
    grave.

           *   *

Therefore seeing ever clearlier that the time has come at last
For one frail man's giant protest, I have summoned up the past
— I have written, since I saw the fatal ring upon her hand,
Plainly all our strange sad story, that the world may understand.

In the long week since I saw it, that clear token of our doom,
I have relived all the stages, seen the sunlight, felt the gloom,
Every scene and every trifle have endeavoured to recall.
I alone knew all the sorrow.   Now the world shall know it all.

I will leave the story written, signed and sealed, within my desk,
Then will rise up fierce for action, calm no longer, statuesque
Now no longer—not a statue, but a living breathing frame
Wild for wrestle with the Author of the sin, the woe, the shame.

Even now I feel within me strange swift heart-throbs of relief,
Somewhat even of exultation, triumph born of deadliest grief;
Even now I see before me as it were with prophet's glance
All the future made the present, known, experienced, in advance.

I will steer into the Atlantic : Fate has wrecked and ruined me—
I will form a last alliance with the thunder of the sea.
Heaven has failed, aye God has failed me—Christ has failed me
    in my need ;
But the sea's heart still is left me, with the sea's heart I will
    plead.

I will steer into the sunset : as that sunset years ago
Bathed the world for me and Annie in its loving golden glow,
As that sunset flashed before us with the radiance of a dream,
Now another spotless sunset shall deliver and redeem.

For this girl—another Annie—now another sunset waits :
Yea, the sunset shall receive her in its fiery golden gates.
All the fairy guards are waiting, far behind the walls of flame ;
For long years they have been waiting for their queen who never
    came.

But their pure queen now is coming ; let the fairy bugles blow !
Let the fairies line the roadway ! let the news fly to and fro !
Let there be a stir, a bustle, through the fairies' wide domain,
For the queen they've lost for ages is returning home again.

Stately, noble, pure and queenly, full of girlish grace and charm,
With God's genius as a sculptor shown in curve of throat and arm,

With God's holier sense of sweetness in her maiden heart made
    known,
She is coming, she for ever is returning to her own.

She, returning, will be with us now for evermore, and bring
As the golden gates she enters such a sudden sense of spring
As on earth we feel when Winter with one foot yet on the wold
Starts and trembles, as the furze-shoots flash their sudden spears
    of gold.

She, returning, will be with us—lo ! the golden sunset waits :
She will enter far within it, far beyond the golden gates.
She will traverse the old region, she its everlasting queen,
With a sovereignty of splendour never witnessed in her mien.

With a sovereignty of sweetness now within the queenly eyes
She will traverse the old region, see the mountain land that lies
Far beyond the fairy borders, which no eye of man has seen,—
She the eternal perfect ruler, she the eternal sinless queen.

Once again the golden sunset—once again, then never more—
Shall flash out with heaven's own brilliance all along the Cornish
    shore.
Here, where Tristram at Tintagel sinned with Iseult at his side,
To the sunset, to the Atlantic, I will bring a sinless bride.

Here, where Arthur's endless vigil of wild sorrow was begun,
I will end all mortal sorrow ; it shall set as sets the sun.
It shall vanish in the sunset, it shall vanish in the sea ;
It shall vanish in the radiance of the sky's immensity.

What the Lord God failed in doing when he placed upon the
    hand
Of the world her ring of wedding, and espoused the sea and land,
I a mortal, I so erring, will accomplish by my might :
I will end the pain of living, pain shall vanish in a night.

Pain shall vanish—for, a mortal, I can show the immortal road
That not even Christ's brave footstep in its fullest grandeur
    showed :
I can add to Jesus' gospel ; I can follow where he went ;
I can bring on earth the silence of a measureless content.

I can take this woman holding as it were within her womb
A vast power of sorrow endless, endless summers' dying bloom,
Endless souls unhinged by anguish, boundless agonies to be,—
I can plunge the mortal mother in the vast womb of the sea.

I can stay a million curses and avert a million pangs :
Grief, men fancied, was immortal—I can blunt grief's deadly
    fangs.
Men will follow where I lead them : I will lead them to the deep,
To the sea of vast oblivion, to the shores of endless sleep.

There all sorrow shall be ended, and the whole race shall atone
For the crime of its creation and revert without a groan,
Nay with one wild hymn of triumph, to the unconscious ecstasy
Of the fields no ploughshare furrows and the unfurrowed shipless
    sea.

M

That was joy and life unfailing, free from conscious life's despair ;
Then the pale moon swam in silence through the sorrowless blue
    air :
Then the soul that gazes downward from the red depths of the sun
Watched the earth, yet saw no evil, for no human deed was done.

That was rapture for creation ! then the golden lonely stars
Tilted not with rays immortal at our mortal prison bars :
Then they saw no prisoner dying on his silent couch,—they heard
Neither battle's shout of triumph nor the lover's whispered word.

Love was waiting to destroy us,—but love had not dawned on
    earth.
All the sea laughed out unconscious, through its voice rang
    thoughtless mirth :
Not the mirth it caught from Venus when she sprang from waves
    that smiled ;
Not the laughter of the lover, but the laughter of the child.

Love was waiting to destroy us,—but as yet the world was free.
Lovers loved not on the ocean for no ships sailed on the sea :
Lovers loved not in the forests, and the lone hills watched the
    moon
Trodden not by feet of lovers ; loveless were the fields of June.

That was peace and pleasure perfect ; that great peace I will
    restore.
Love shall vanish from the mountains, love shall die out on the
    shore.
I, the preacher of the gospel of despair and boundless gloom,
Will restore the world its silence, and its empire to the tomb.

Men shall follow my example : step by step the world will cease
To run madly after pleasure, and will long alone for peace.
Then the cornfields will be weed-grown : who will care to reap the
    corn
When man views himself with hatred and the whole of life with
    scorn ?

House by house the towns will crumble, tower by tower the
    shrines will fall,
Till a measureless cold silence broods serenely over all.
Man shall rise at last in anger, man shall utterly disdain
God, whose empire without limit means illimitable pain.

Man shall wreak at last his vengeance on the Power that bade
    him be,
Sending man without a compass to explore a shoreless sea ;
Sending man to climb a summit where the white mists never part,
In his brain a doubt eternal and despair within his heart.

Man shall wreak at last his vengeance—as I wreak my vengeance,
    I,
Steering out into the darkness, for the sun has left the sky ;
Bearing with me this one woman—would God lower her and
    deprave ?
Her at least he shall not conquer—her at least my hand shall
    save.

Though I could not save the mother, is not she the mother now,
With the same young strange pure sweetness in the eyes and on
    the brow?

All the long sad years have vanished—Lo! love rises from its
    grave :
I may save from black pollution her I would have died to save.

Not in London shall she perish : now our bridal couch shall be
Pure and sweet and holy and stainless, even the holy and stainless
    sea.
She whom once I loved in London, where I loved her for an
    hour,
Shall be mine in love immortal, far beyond Fate's lurid power.

This is nobler, this ends better than the sad old tale began ;
This is worthier of my passion, this is worthier of a man.
Now the tender night is coming, and the stars will light our way
To the room where death is bridegroom, not the room where
    once we lay.

I am death her perfect bridegroom, we are on the lonely deep :
Now the night eternal waits us, we have many an hour for sleep ;
Sweet long hours for sleep, my darling—there's no footstep at the
    door !
Nay, the winds and waves shall guard us, we are many a league
    from shore.

We are lonely at last together, we have left the adulterous land :
Lo! our solemn marriage-chamber, lo! our spotless couch at
    hand.
You and I are all alone, love—mortal sounds have died away ;
Hear the stars' song to the ocean ! hear the wind's voice to the
    spray !

Lest our deep calm should be troubled, lest our marriage should
    be marred,
God has sent the unnumbered armies of the deathless stars to
    guard :
That our rapture may be endless and our souls past waking one
He has darkened earth for ever, he has slain the intrusive sun.

Lest I find you all too lovely, he has sent the moon to show
With her soft light for the first time your uncovered breast of
    snow :
Lest I scorn all flowers for ever when your first kiss startles me,
He has left the flowers on land, love—he has set us on the sea.

Lest the roses all be envious, he has made your mouth a rose ;
He has left a thousand blossoms on the cliff-sides in repose,
He has given ephemeral fragrance to the flowers, ephemeral bliss,
He will make the rose eternal in the sweetness of your kiss.

Lest the thought of an invasion of our joy should e'er intrude,
Any thought of old dead cities, he has given us solitude :
Lest a dream of other beings should bring sadness to your face,
He has ended other life, love, he has slain the human race.

He has had at last great mercy, he has given us bliss divine,
Perfect death for you and me, love—life in death, for you are
    mine.
Ours will be the last embrace, love : on this white-waved ocean-
    plain
One last rapture superhuman shall end superhuman pain.

All the rapture of the passion that from Eve's first soft kiss ran
Like a torrent, like a fire-flood, through the throbbing veins of
    man,
All the raptures of old history, shall be gathered into ours,
As the rose resumes the fragrance of a million nameless flowers.

That is mightiest compensation—thus to loose within our veins
The full torrent of past passion, and to fix the past in chains :
Thus to bind the world for ever, but to set two lovers free,—
Then to send a world's kiss pressing through your single mouth
    to me.

This is noblest compensation—to put out the human race,
But to leave the love-light burning through your eyes and in my
    face
—Thus to let us feel our oneness, I with you, and you with me,
And your oneness with the starlight, and my oneness with the sea.

Place this once, my stainless darling, your pure lips upon my own :
These at least are wholly sinless, these at least are mine alone.
Now let sweet death seal the marriage ! when two souls are one at
    last
Then death's darkness is not darkness, for the power of death is
    past.

Not to-morrow shall we, waking, hear the wheels of London roll,
You with sin's kiss on your whiteness, I with madness in my soul :
Nay, for ever now around us let the vast night's curtains be !
We are safe within the darkness ; we are safe within the sea.

THE FEAST OF LANTERNS.

THE FEAST OF LANTERNS.

I.

THE LANTERNS.

ONE evening, weary in brain and sad of heart,
　　I strolled along a sea-front—watched the tide,
Saw golden sunset glitter, then depart
　　While raven darkness spread her mantle wide.

But in that hour my soul was left alone,
　　Unloved of night, unsolaced of the sea :
I turned aside, and lo ! a garden shone
　　With glittering lanterns strung from tree to tree.

I entered, and through all my heart there rushed
　　The sense of youth and gladness once again :
Half pleased, yet half in very truth I blushed
　　To think how slight a salve cures human pain !

I had been sad at heart, but here was light,
　　Warmth, colour—pain had loosed its strangling hold :—
The dark trees framed more star-lamps than the night ;
　　Their branches flashed with gems, or burned with gold.

Then, in that mood in which one takes account
　　Of little things and lets all great cares flee,
I let my gaze from lawn to terrace mount,
　　From bush illumed to lamp-bedizened tree.

My fancy revelled in the fiery gleams
　　Of Eastern colour from the lanterns flung ;
There mixed a thousand artists' wayward dreams,
　　Love-tales unheard and Epics never sung.

There crimson mandarins put emerald flocks
　　Of huge Satanic cranes to shameful flight,
And gorgeous fishes cruised amid blue rocks,
　　Golden, with eyes whence flashed unearthly light.

Pale black-capped soldiers, massed in threatening groups,
　　Loomed fierce upon the lanterns,—pig-tailed kings,
And executioners, red-handed troops,
　　And giant butterflies with jewelled wings.

Knives raised from severed necks yet dripped with gore ;
　　Delicious damsels, dainty, almond-eyed,
Ogled their swains ; upon a yellow shore
　　Strange painted junks lay basking in their pride.

Grim hieroglyphics, Chinese down-strokes, meant
　　No doubt, " I love you—all my heart is thine ! "
—While over all flowed soft the mystic scent
　　The night-wind culls from heliotrope and pine.

　　　　　*　　　　　　*

Then 'mid that maze of sweet bewildering light
    The fears that silence lovers fled away,
And young hearts gathered courage from the night
    Who found no words nor courage in the day.

And there were shadowy places, bowers apart,
    Where lovers, quitting lamp-land for awhile,
Might interchange the thoughts of heart and heart,
    With ardour plead, or vanquish with a smile.

There some who had dreamed for years yet never won
    The gift of one soft tress, one treasured flower,
Tongue-tied beneath the harsh gaze of the sun,
    Found passionate words within the kindly bower.

And lips too coy by day to yield their fill
    Of sweetest ecstasy and pure delight
Bent forward eager answering lips to thrill,
    Full of the balm and magic of the night.

Eyes which by day were cowards were braver now
    And dared within the shadowy bowers to gleam,
Full of the light that makes the lover vow
    That but for love's light star-land were a dream !

And tender tongues, sweet cowards alas ! by day,
    Won from the stars the mandate to be bold,
Heedless what jewels of speech they flung away,
    What lovely word-gems of seductive gold.

For round about the thousand lanterns gleamed ;
   Upon the leafy boughs they gently swung :
Of fairy-land all fervent young hearts dreamed,
   And old hearts dreamed of days when they were young.

Then underneath two elms whose verdant gloom
   Shadowed a mimic stage, a play began.
The armoured hero tossed his snowy plume :
   The villain of the piece disclosed his plan.

A play wins magic from the soft night air,
   Steals glamour from surroundings such as these ;
The lovely village-maid seems twice as fair
   Beneath the actual shadow of living trees.

The courtly dame of passionate romance
   Seems twice as courtly, more romantic far,
When o'er real leaves her lover's steps advance
   And through real branches peeps the evening star.

Moreover sombre deeds that dye the soul
   Crimson, dark horrors fleeing from the light,
Seem twice as grim when actors play their *rôle*
   Beneath the sombre ceiling of the night.

All is so real—we watch no more a part
   That some mere actor, aping passion, plays :
We feel the wild love throb through Romeo's heart
   And Shakespeare's Juliet thrills us as we gaze.

I gazed—the strange spell seized me, and I felt
  While in the background countless lanterns gleamed
As if before some sacred shrine I knelt
  Or in Art's holiest temple gazed and dreamed.

Music was rapture—notes that ne'er before
  Had aught of magic power, creative might,
Now struck the airs, each note a tiny oar
  Urging the soul's bark towards unknown delight.

The universe seemed made for love alone ;
  All men were lovers, women all were sweet :
Sorrow was but a phase to be outgrown
  And death a phantom cringing at our feet.

II.

A VOICE FROM THE SEA.

THE night waxed onward—still the lanterns shone
  Swung, gently still, by slightly freshening air ;
Still love was king and pleasure held its own
  Untired, and still the daring wooed the fair.

Still in that magic garden life seemed good
  And still from young lips rang their silvery glee
When I through bosky paths in thoughtful mood
  Moved slowly forth and sought the silent sea.

Not far it was—the garden sheltered lay,
  A sweet enchanted stormless lamplit spot ;
Yet hardly a stone's throw forth a waste of grey
  Stretched, hearing love's soft laugh, but heeding not.

No lanterns flashed upon the sombre deep,
  No throne of pleasure stood exalted there,
But stirring as it were in troubled sleep
  The windless ocean murmured to the air :

" I hear the sounds of joyance—through dark leaves
  Uncounted tiny meteor-lanterns shine ;
The earth is gladdened, or my ear deceives :
  Yet what abysmal loneliness is mine !

" No stars to-night through all the cloud-draped halls
  Of heaven shall glitter, nor shall laughter be
To-night within the black sky's boundless walls
  Save only mine, the laughter of the sea."

I heard, and as I heard my spirit thrilled
  Moved deep within me—from the sea there came
A sudden sense of mighty power that filled
  My spirit with might and joy without a name.

No more the scent of heliotrope and pine
  Suggested love's soft hour and passion's glee ;
My nostrils drank the scent, the scent divine,
  That gives to man the strange soul of the sea.

And, as I drank the scent, my soul grew great
  And amorous for the sea's embrace and strong ;
Then through the starless dark heaven's cloudy gate
  Came the first cadence of the night-wind's song :—

"One *fête*, O sea ! and are not thousands thine,
  When through the heights and depths of purple space
The frenzied spears of forked red lightning shine
  And when the pale ships shudder at thy face ?

" One mortal *fête*, one garden's joyous bowers
 Wherein swift-hearted lovers urge their claims—
Lo ! theirs are one night's perishable flowers,
 Thine are the golden stars' immortal flames.

" *Fêtes* thou hast watched on balmier shores than these
 Beneath a softer heaven, where gentler night
Darkens the myrtle-groves and orange trees
 And where fair women's eyes flash lovelier light.

" Where are the lovers who beside thy waves
 Exchanged love's vows a thousand years ago ?
Thy waters wash above their lampless graves :
 Above their summer haunts thy wild waves flow.

" *Fêtes* thou hast watched on ships that through the deep
 Urge venturous keels—then changing light to gloom
Hast bade the music pause, the dancers sleep
 No wakeful slumber in their cold vast tomb.

" Man is but mortal but, immortal sea,
 Beyond all words thine heart and mine are strong :
Thou hast the music of eternity
 Within thy silence, I within my song."

Then, as the wind's song ceased, from cloud on cloud
 The sudden spears of lightning flashed their gleams ;
The thunder pealed above the plains unploughed ;
 Far in the past seemed passion's languid dreams.

For now a larger passion shook my soul
   Swayed by the prowess of the stormy night :
I laughed to hear the rising breakers roll,
   Watching the echoing coast-line fringed with white.

The storm-wind and the sea were holding there
   Majestic parley, their wild hearts were one :—
The lightning's fiery radiance thrilled the air,
   The midnight blackness that defies the sun.

And through it all I mortal was a part
   Of the immortal—time had ceased to be.
The mighty sea's was as the storm-wind's heart :
   The storm-wind's soul was boisterous with the sea.

All was forgotten save the strife I saw,
   The strife that hurls the doomed ships to their goal :
With rapture deeper even than deepest awe
   I saw revealed the ocean's deathless soul ;

The soul that though man's race to-day might die
   Would still hold parley with the storm, the night,
And still through limitless eternity
   Worship the gloom and battle with the light.

III.

A SILENT morn—the storm had wholly passed,
 The sunless ocean rested still and grey ;
I sought the garden paths, the lawns green-grassed,
 Where last night's feastful hours had slipped away.

Ah ! in one night wild autumn's hand had flung
 The spoil of months upon the sodden ground :
The trees where last night's graceful lanterns swung
 Seemed now in sombre funeral robes enwound.

Their leaves that yesterday bore summer's green
 And made believe that June's sky still was bright
Were robbed to-day of all their lustrous sheen,
 Stained to disastrous russet in a night.

Upon the lawns the brown sere leaves were strewn,
 Mixed with some scattered lanterns' coloured shreds ;
Bright paper globes that mocked the golden moon
 Last night lay tattered on wet paths and beds.

178

Among the heliotrope the mandarins
  In hopeless wild forlorn confusion lay,
Blending their gorgeous reds and vivid greens
  With purple flowers in desolate array.

Where last night's graceful Juliet moved divine
  A few damp planks and boards neglected frowned,
And sombre seemed the lawn's dark fringe of pine
  That last night heard soft amorous laughter sound.

Then through my soul there ran a sudden dread,
  An icy terror—" Can this horror be ?
Must soon all bright and joyous things be dead ?
  Is nought immortal save the storm and sea ?

" Is even the sea itself with all its waves
  Mortal ? Hath time who slays each human form
The power to dig for oceans monstrous graves,
  The strength to hush the trumpets of the storm ?

" Is there one Spirit who gazing from on high
  Sees planet after planet reach its goal,
Who sees each star within the starry sky
  Enact its part, and every human soul,—

" Who then, the farce being ended, says to all,
  To last night's lovers and to moon and sun,
'The play is over—let the curtain fall !
  Pass into darkness, for your hour is done' ? "

KING SOLOMON.

KING SOLOMON.

When at the last the great King's heart grew weary,
   When pleasure's wild impassioned reign was done,
When laughter of bright lips rang dull and dreary,
   When sadness veiled the stars and veiled the sun,

Then with grim Death the great King thus debated :
   "The end is drawing near, lift up thine eyes,"
Said Death ; "through all these long years I have waited,
   But now my patient keen spear claims its prize."

" But, Death, the world is mine, its every season—
   I am the lord of winter and of spring ;
If one flower failed to obey me, it were treason."
   Then answered Death: " I also am a King.

" The flowers of all the flower-filled world obey me ;
   They smile one hour upon thee half in scorn,
Yet not for all thy wealth will they gainsay me :
   I steal the rubies from the brow of morn.

" Where is thy last month's concubine ? thou hast missed her ?
   The dark-brown eyes, the soft lips' fragrant bloom—
With lips more masterful than thine I kissed her,
   Then built our bridal chamber in the tomb.

" Arise.   The sun and stars were thine, the glory
    Of empire measureless as morning's light :
Green plains and forests dark and mountains hoary ;
    Rest in the day and rapture in the night.

" Thy throne was molten gold, with ivory blended,
    A work of which no craftsman's heart had dreamed :
On the six steps by which thy foot ascended
    Twelve golden lions, maned with terror, gleamed.

" Beside the throne two lions even more massive,
    Sculptured in silent gold, yet seemed to say,
' If man's heart trembles while our strength rests passive
    Earth's soul must shudder when we pant for prey.'

" Sheba's fair queen with costliest presents sought thee ;
    Thy wisdom through the wide earth won renown :
Kings did thee homage,—Ophir's gold they brought thee ;
    The golden sun was envious of thy crown.

" The moon was envious in her pearly whiteness
    Of women whose soft whiteness gladdened thee :
Through pitchy night, or under noontide's brightness,
    Thy countless strong ships coursed from sea to sea.

" Horses they brought thee from far Egypt's regions,
    Proud-nostrilled, fiery, many a flawless form ;
Steeds fit to mount thine horsemen's mustering legions,
    Maned like the night and footed like the storm.

" Thy chariots gathered in each chariot-city
   Flashed back the sunlight from their wheels of gold :
Where David's splashed through blood-pools without pity
   Through flower-strewn streets thy cars of triumph rolled.

" Not heaven itself had stars enough to greet thee—
   Bright India's birds for thee must rob the skies,
Spread star-besprinkled plumes, and raise to meet thee
   Their banners glorious with a thousand eyes.

" David's fierce wars and warrior-deeds were over ;
   The light of peace on all the glad land fell :
Thine eyes were ever soft eyes of a lover,
   Though sombre David's eyes took fire from hell.

" Thou hadst no need of mad adultery's rapture
   For thy strong men sent forth through land on land
Brought thee, through fair gifts won or kingly capture,
   Forms by some love-god's passionate genius planned.

" The women of all the realm were thine. Didst covet
   Some girl with hair that mocked the raven's wing ?
At night her mouth was thine, thy lips might love it,
   And she might say, ' I worship thee, O King ! '

" At morn, if thou didst weary of her embraces,
   Let the joy wane with dawning of the light !
For thee another of countless sweet girl-faces
   Rose with the stars, resplendent on the night.

"The joy men seek and many a life foregoes it,
  The pressure of virgin lips by no man won,
Was thine a thousand times—the dark night knows it
  That for thy sake craved respite from the sun.

"To thee the God of David seemed austerer
  Than gentler gods of nations round thy throne :
To thee the white-armed Ashtaroth was dearer
  Than the stern Lord whom Sinai's peaks enthrone.

"The women-gods of nations round thy borders
  To thee were lovelier than Jehovah's form :
Upon the hill-sides temples at thine orders
  Rose to the gods of starlight or the storm.

"Thy soul was full of artist-dreams and fancies ;
  Thou ponderedst on the tales thy women told,
On Midianitish lore and strange romances
  Of passionate gods who ruled in kingdoms old.

"But now the end has come.   Lift up thy glances—
  Glances that shook the earth and shook the sea.
O King, a mightier step than thine advances :
  Tremble,—as all the world once quailed at thee."

                    *   *

Then Solomon : "O Death with gaze tremendous,
  What lamp shall light me when I leave the sun ? "
And Death, with voice than thunder more stupendous :
  "All stars I extinguish, King, save only one."

Then Solomon : " O Death with lance that quivers,
  What cup shall proffer me my costly wine ? "
And Death : " O King, within my realm are rivers ;
  The right to lap their black waves shall be thine."

Then Solomon : " O bitter Death, thus leaving
  The land of plenty, what food shall I take ? "
And Death : " Thy soul will hunger not, receiving
  Each day one loaf of memory's bread to break."

Then Solomon : " O Death, what change of raiment
  Shall I select from all my priceless store ? "
And Death : " Thou hast robbed the world, the time for pay-
    ment
  Approaches—take thy winding-sheet, no more."

Then Solomon : " Of queens whose eyes mocked morning
  Which shall I choose for mistress of the night ? "
And Death : " The faithfullest—but with this warning,
  Find, if thou canst, one woman who was not light."

Then Solomon : " On what couch shall I slumber,
  I who with many a white-limbed love have lain ? "
And Death : " Thy loves have been so many in number
  That surely to sleep single will be gain ? "

Then Solomon : " And how long shall I tarry
  Within the darkness that man's spirit fears,
The gloom where bodiless souls eat not nor marry
  Nor drink nor slumber ? " Death : " Three thousand years."

     *   *

Four times the great King's loneliness was broken,
　　Four times a spirit in those three thousand years
Hovering approached him, and a word was spoken
　　That rang like thunder in the great King's ears.

Four times a spirit he once had loved addressed him ;
　　Four times that spirit forsook him as in scorn :
Four times a spirit whose arms had once caressed him
　　Left him in darkness, crying, " I love the morn ! "

The first time thus it happed.　He saw swift-sailing
　　On starlike wings through night's perpetual gloom
A spirit whose glory and loveliness unfailing
　　Had sweeter been to him than summer's bloom.

She on the bridal night with queenly laughter
　　Had said : " Bestow a gift on me, O King—
A gift that may recall through all the hereafter,
　　In life's dim winter, passion's peerless spring."

And he : " Ask what thou wilt.　The world of flowers
　　Is mine, and the underworld of jewelled gleams.
O love, shall blood-bright rubies gem thy bowers ?
　　O queen, shall star-bright diamonds haunt thy dreams ?

" Shall Hiram's vessels bring thee gold unmeasured
　　From Tyre, from Sidon ?　Shall the purple sea
Yield up the noblest pearls its depths have treasured ?
　　Shall looms of Edom weave rich robes for thee ?

" Thou art the fairest of far Moab's daughters.
  For this thy first kiss what gift shall I bring ?
Ores from the mountains, amber from the waters ?
  Speak thou, O queen—command thy slave, the King."

And she with eyes of more than mortal splendour,
  Eyes whose bright glance might lead the sun astray,
Smiling had said : " In love's supreme surrender
  My heart is thine, thy will I must obey ;

" I am thy slave—thou art my lord, my master,—
  Thine am I from this moment to my grave ;
Yet woman am I—my desire is vaster
  Than starlit night, more hungry than the wave.

" To-night take all my beauty—it is fairer,
  They say in Moab, than the day-dawn bright :
A royal crown is mine, win thou the wearer ;
  Win from me all thou canst of strange delight.

" Yet grant me this, O King—one thing I covet ;
  In Moabitish blood desire runs high :
Thou fondlest my white hand,—thou sayest, ' I love it !'
  Place in that hand the rainbow from the sky."

The great King laughed.   " O queen, the rainbow's splendour
  In that white hand of thine thou yet shalt hold—
Its gleaming hues, its changing tints most tender,
  Its red and green, its lilac and its gold."

Then by his magic spells the great King, knowing
   Secrets revealed to him on earth alone,
Created opals—thus for e'er bestowing
   The rainbow's charm and glamour on a stone.

           *   *

But now she said : " The opal's charm has vanished ;
   My soul has grown beyond such gauds as these.
Listen, thou King to night's deep darkness banished ;
   On earth new sunlight shines on lands and seas.

" I am the spirit of Freedom—thou the enslaving
   Strong King of all the world liest chained and bound.
Thou mayest not even see the green grass waving ;
   Thou mayest not hear stern Sparta's trumpet sound.

" From Asia once again harsh slavery threatens ;
   The dateless future on a thin thread hangs :
Asia's tumultuous vast host hourly greatens,
   One monstrous serpent with unmeasured fangs.

" Three hundred heroes in the pass are posted
   With keen eyes gazing on the silvery sea,
The sea that guards the fair land golden-coasted :—
   Man's history pauses at Thermopylæ.

" Lo ! time is poised upon a moment breathless :
   Of centuries Leonidas is lord.
Three hundred deaths shall make three hundred deathless ;
   Ten thousand years are balanced on a sword.

" As by a hair all Europe's fate is dangling :
  ' Draw back,' saith darkness to the golden morn—
' Draw back, give place, while Xerxes' hand is strangling
  The neck of Freedom, in its iron scorn.'

" Five hundred years have passed since in thy palace,
  O Solomon, my love I gave to thee :
Our rainbow-opals circled passion's chalice ;
  Now Freedom's rainbow-circlet crowns the sea.

" I, once a slave to all thy royal caprices,
  Am now to Freedom only chainless thrall
For Freedom's touch enslaving, yet releases ;
  At Freedom's voice the inveterate fetters fall.

" Now, while pale Europe shrinks from regal capture,
  With brave Leonidas I pause to see
How fearless death may lead to deathless rapture
  And time pay tribute to eternity."

She spoke—the King remained alone and weeping,
  But she flew forth to watch the unequal fight
That left three hundred in the dark pass sleeping,
  Their foreheads crowned with everlasting light.

*   *

Again five hundred years of darkness, lighted
  By the faint radiance of that single star,
Passed o'er the mighty King in gloom benighted,
  Closed in by past deeds, as by bolt and bar.

Then through the gloom he marked a spirit approaching ;
   Before her feet aside the mist-wreaths fell :
Her golden wings upon the dark encroaching
   Lit up like sudden lamps the vaults of hell.

A thousand years ago (she then a maiden
   Of Ammon, he great Israel's peerless lord)
He had said, his kingly heart with passion laden,
   " Choose what thou wilt—then trust my unfailing sword."

And she, within whose hair the stars mistaking
   Its blackness for sweet night aspired to rest,
Said, " Of all jewels of the earth-gods' wondrous making
   I love the deep-green emerald far the best.

" Yet bring me not the emerald's transient lustre ;
   Plant a vast forest round about our throne,
Within whose leafage the sun's rays may muster
   Legions of emeralds nobler than the stone ! "

So Solomon with ready heart had ordered
   For her the dark-haired amorous white-browed queen
A palace to be built, by dense woods bordered,
   Where living emeralds flashed their leafy green.

But now to-day she said : " O King, low-lying
   Within the darkness, helpless in the gloom,
Upon the earth the sullen night is dying !
   A living light has flashed upon the tomb !

" A nobler reign than thine is now beginning :
　A mighty Lord, descended, King, from thee,
Shall make an end of lust and wrath and sinning,—
　By love's voice hush the thunder-throated sea.

" Rome's empire now through all the world extending
　Recalls and yet exceeds thine empire old,
But this King's empire, when pale Rome's is ending,
　Boundless, shall storm the sunset's gates of gold.

" Women shall seek him—aye, throughout the eras—
　But by sweet pureness are his victories won.
While past kings' dreams dissolve like mist-chimeras
　His kingdom shall outstay the flagging sun.

" The skies shall hear the last low roll of thunder
　That wearies on the horizon's pallid verge ;
Beside the lessening waves man's heart shall wonder
　At the last effort of the worn-out surge :

" The very stars with fragments golden-gleaming
　May strew the heavens, the night drown out the day,
The moon may cease to set the green woods dreaming,—
　Christ's timeless kingdom cannot pass away.

Within his kingdom clasping all things human
　In deathless clasp of sympathy divine
A fairer throne than thy throne waits for woman,
　A kinglier love, great Solomon, than thine."

　　　　*　　　　　*

In fifteen hundred years the shadows shifted ;
  More light flashed downward from the single star
His weary brow once more the great King lifted,—
  He saw a spirit approaching from afar.

A queen he recognised whose golden tresses
  Through the Eastern night shone fairer than the sun
In the old lost hours of mirth and love-caresses,
  A wife in Midian's mountain-regions won.

" And art thou come to cheer my lonely slumber,
  To be once more my light ? " the great King said :
" I, once the lord of palaces past number,
  Have now no pillow for thy golden head ! "

The sweet ghost answered : " Past all power of telling
  Is the great change within my spirit wrought
Since by those Eastern fountains upward welling
  We wandered, mingling queenly and kingly thought.

" O King, my soul has grown beyond thy dreaming ;
  Thine harem's backward blossoms all have blown :
The eyes that once were stars upon thee gleaming
  Are now as suns to lands thou hast not known.

" A mighty power beyond the Western waters,
  England, has risen—a land where all are free.
My heart is now as hearts of England's daughters
  Full of the passion of the chainless sea.

" Work have I now to do—work vast, undying ;
  I may not share with thee thy timeless sleep :
have to watch, on my keen sight relying,
  A mighty fleet whose sails are on the deep.

" Beyond thy dreams of love my soul has risen ;
  I am thy slave, thy love-crowned queen, no more !
Rest thou for ever in thy lonely prison ;
  I am as free as waves that kiss the shore.

" Lo ! from the South a giant fleet approaches ;
  Slaves are they who man it, and a king who sends :
On English waters their lewd flag encroaches ;
  On me the Armada's destiny depends.

" Fate has bestowed on me the power of hurling
  Upon the Armada all the ocean's might,
Wild winds and thunders and white waters whirling :
  Woman I was—I am the spirit of night !

" Fate's hand has stolen the stars of night for crowning
  My forehead—starless yet my wreath shall be
That Philip's fleet may perish, darkness drowning
  A godless host in hell-depths of the sea.

" That is my work, O King—not now to sunder
  The self-forged chains that hold thee powerless there
But forth to hurl the lightning and the thunder,
  Queen of the storm and sovereign of the air."

*   *

Ere long once more the lonely watch was broken—
   A spirit approached on dawn-pink pinions borne,
Then, ere the great King's doubtful word was spoken,
   Said : " King, behold in me the spirit of morn !

" Dost thou remember me the Hittite maiden
   Of whose blue eyes thou didst one morning say,
' The sunlit heights beside them are mist-laden ;
   Twin sovereigns are they of the golden day ! '

" Ages have passed—behold ! in England rises
   The mightiest poet whom man's race shall hear,—
He who can penetrate all hearts' disguises
   And make all history's darkest moments clear.

" Him have I now to aid, smiting asunder
   Old shackles, pouring through his song supreme
Whereat all time to come shall pause in wonder
   The force of truth, the sweetness of a dream.

" Woman I was—I am the spirit of morning
   And morning's breath in Shakespeare's song shall be ;
Strength as of dawn, when rose-flushed peaks give warning,
   And boundless light as of the shoreless sea.

" Not Milcah, Tirzah, Asenath—no longer
   Our dark-eyed maidens hold man's spirit bound ;
Man worships even far sweeter souls and stronger,
   Souls whom the poet of mankind has crowned.

" England to-day takes up the chant of the ages,
 And through that chant rings woman's rallying cry :
Within her heart a blossoming hope assuages
 Her long despair, her voiceless agony.

" Thou in the East didst hold our spirits fettered :
 Prisoned we were, though golden were the walls !
Wast thou for one slave's soft kiss truly bettered,
 Thou, loveless tyrant of a thousand thralls ?

" Now in the West our agelong bonds are broken.
 Was Desdemona modelled from a slave ?
Could any word by mightiest monarch spoken
 Curb Portia's spirit,—or control the wave ?

" The sea's force in the hearts of England's daughters
 From tyrant-kings for ever sets them free.
Thy sceptre swayed the hills, but not the waters :
 The desert was thy footstool, not the sea.

" The sea is Shakespeare's, and his land's, for ever ;
 The sea, the stars, the everlasting sun,
The passionate heart of love that wearies never—
 These all are England's, till all time be done."

* *

Again five hundred years—the star seemed nearer :
 Its golden portals filled with fiery light
Flashed till the dense surrounding gloom grew clearer ;
 A gleam of hope shot radiance through the night.

Hope !   For three thousand years the King, despairing,
  In woe profound and darkness' depths had lain :
Can hope whose soul is love, whose breath is daring,
  Light up those lampless soundless deeps again ?

Then starlike—even as if the star, creating
  Its fairy spirit of brightness, from afar
Had sent her—came on wings unhesitating
  A spirit whose glance was radiant as a star.

Then Solomon remembered, slowly raising
  The shadowy curtains of three thousand years,
A maiden passing forth from love, and gazing
  One moment back with dark eyes full of tears.

She had given the King one month of kingly pleasure,
  One month,—and then had passed into the gloom :
But in that month her soul with all its treasure
  Had blossomed, all its wealth of scent and bloom.

She had loved the King, she just a captive maiden—
  He ruler of the earth, of sea and land.
She gave her soul to him, with sweetness laden :
  He took the flower,—then dropped it from his hand.

But now, though vast strange centuries intervening
  Had done their varying tasks, then waned and fled
She, apprehending love's eternal meaning,
  Had sought the King among the living dead.

She spirit-ruler of the star whose brightness
    Had dared to face the midnight's sombre scorn
Now, pure as mountain-snow's ethereal whiteness,
    Came whispering words of sweet hope newly born.

"Rise!" said she: "time is nought, and life is vaster
    Than all the swift-winged ways and moods of time.
Not death, but love, is all the ages' master,—
    Lord even of hell, star-garlanded, sublime.

"A thousand hearts have failed thee. Yet, immortal,
    A mightier love than theirs pulsates through one.
Lift up thine eyes. Through morning's golden portal
    Rolls slowly forth the chariot of the sun."

Then Solomon arose.—The star receded;
    Its task accomplished, that pale lamp might die:
But in the East its lustre was not needed,
    For love's majestic morning lit the sky.

JOHN HENRY NEWMAN

AND

VICTOR HUGO.

JOHN HENRY NEWMAN AND VICTOR HUGO.

(JOHN HENRY NEWMAN : born Feb. 21st, 1801, died Aug. 11th, 1890.
VICTOR HUGO : born Feb. 26th, 1802, died May 22nd, 1885.)

WHILE all men's hearts with new-born hope were fed,
    Hope in the morning, sweet faith in the sun,
Hope that dark tyrannous ages all were dead,
    That reigns of kings and reigns of priests were done ;

While all men's eyes beheld the morning light
    Red in the skies, but blood-red over France,—
While all men dreamed that now the starless night
    Had quailed before the high sun's fiery glance ;

While all men dreamed that now on Europe's plains
    Untinged with blood might wave the untrodden rye,—
While Revolution's forehead red with stains
    Confronted unabashed the sunlit sky,

Two sunlike spirits arose—on each the doom
    Of endless love, redemptive of their race :
And unto one the sweet morn's light was gloom,
    And one's eyes looked the strong sun in the face.

To one the light of morn was but a dream ;
　　His heart was with the ages past and dead :
The sunshine seemed a pale deceptive gleam,
　　And Freedom's sword was soiled with ominous red.

His hands groped backward through blind ways and strange,
　　Seeking to grasp the Cross ; his eyes yearned back :
His thoughts that moved within a narrow range
　　Guided his feet along a flowerless track.

Born in an age when thought had risen to smite
　　All chains and fetters from the soul of man,
Born at the morn, he rested in the night,
　　Turned from thought's sea to where thought's stream began.

The stars were more to him—the stars that gleamed
　　Leading wise men along a desert way—
Than the great sun whose glory round him beamed ;
　　The shadowy night was lovelier than the day.

True, noble of heart he was—all men loved well
　　Our English Newman, English to the last.
Rome tempted, tempted subtly, and he fell :
　　Yet from his heart the sweet love never passed.

Still was there something alway in his soul
　　Of English greatness, still his soul was free :
Rome's thunders never wholly hushed the roll
　　Of stormier thunders, thundering from the sea.

　　　　　*　　　　　*

But on the other's soul the morning gleamed.
  Born at the century's dawn, for him the night
Was as a far-off past whereof some dreamed
  While he dreamed only of the golden light.

For him when Revolution's thunders spoke
  It was as if a thousand reigns were done,—
Man freed for ever from night's fruitless yoke
  And servant only of morning and the sun.

All hopes and joys and passions of the race
  Were his to sing, were his in soul to share :
He saw the sun-bright form of Freedom chase
  Gaunt Slavery's form to its last sunless lair.

He saw man's soul as man's soul is to be ;
  Upon the necks of kings and popes he trod :
Man's serfs and thralls in love's name he set free,
  And broke man's idols in the name of God.

Woman he saw, not as she is to-day,
  Man's slave, man's harlot, with the streets for home,
But as she will be when men's hearts obey
  Love's nobler law, in happier years to come.

Lightning of anger flashed along his strain ;
  Through resonant verse the loud song-thunder broke
Yet had he pity for a child's least pain —
  Through him the very heart of childhood spoke.

Pity he had for kings, for all who erred,
    For tyrants, for the ravening souls that slew ;
Aye, tenderest pity for even each captive bird
    That pines for deep green woods and skies of blue.

The eternal love to him was God supreme ;
    The love that dwells behind the sombre skies,
In woman's heart, in woman's passionate dream,—
    The God whose sunlight shines in sinless eyes.

When loudest fell the cataracts of the waves
    And thunder pealed from heaven's exalted dome
Fearless he faced the stormy God who paves
    His floors with shipwreck and his path with foam.

Nature was his—the solemn starlit night ;
    The winds that range the echoing hills for prey ;
Sunrise upon the waters golden-bright ;
    The rose whose beauty triumphs for a day.

And love was his to sing—fair beauty's rose
    Triumphant through wild hours of centuries long :
While through the heart of man love's strange thrill goes
    The heart of man shall love the poet's song.

While on the earth green grows the tender grass
    Each amorous springtide, while on flower and tree
Love scatters jewels as the seasons pass,
    While love's eyes steal their sapphire from the sea ;

While on the mountains the eternal snows
  Gleam white as on the world's first birthday morn,
While first love's kiss is fragrant as the rose,
  While passion laughs the thought of death to scorn;

While other Esmeraldas still arise
  With summer's flower-sweet darkness in their hair,
While once more Doña Sol's imperious eyes
  Bid pale Hernani worship—and despair;

While beauty still is unto man the chief
  Of all things, sweeter than the dream of power,
Shaming with deathless hues the thorns of grief,
  The tints that blush and perish in the flower;

While woman's beauty still is crown of Art,
  The one thing worshipful, the one thing pure,
All loveliness that wrought on Hugo's heart
  In Hugo's song shall blossom and endure.

*   *

Another century dawns,—the thought of each
  Therein beyond all doubt shall have its day:
To some the churchman's cloistered life shall preach,
  And some the poet's stormier heart shall sway.

Some who love best the sunlight filtering through
  Stained glass shall seek with Newman shadowy fanes,
And some with Hugo's spirit shall seek the blue
  Bright sun-kissed sea's illimitable plains.

Aye, some shall dream with Hugo on the waves
    And seek with him the sunlit road to God,
And some with Newman, seeking starlit graves,
    Shall tread the thorn-strewn paths that dead saints trod.

Some souls shall worship where the wild wind reaps
    Its fruitless harvest from the fields of foam,
And some where time is chained and progress sleeps
    Within the walls of immemorial Rome.

Some souls shall deem, deep-moved by Newman's thought,
    The ardent passion of his eager brain,
That England—sea-zoned England—can be brought
    Beneath the yoke of haughty Rome again.

And some, whose hearts the great French poet stirs,
    Shall dream that Paris in the end shall be
The wide world's centre—all man's worship hers,
    And hers the wealth of many a far-searched sea ;

That in the end when all men's minds are one
    And all men's hearts love's uninvaded home
Love's reign, already in his heart begun,
    Shall be complete in Paris, not in Rome.

Some hearts shall dream with Newman that the ghost
    Of love, the ghost the Roman Church allows,
Is fittest bride for man aspiring most,
    Man's purest helpmate, most seductive spouse ;

Deeming that human love must ever err
　　When passion through it throbs with mighty force,—
Not seeing woman, but the shadow of her,—
　　Deeming love's rapture senseless half, half coarse ;

Holding that ever far beyond the skies
　　Must love accomplish its diviner dream,
And that the light that flashes from the eyes
　　Of woman draws from hell its magic gleam.

Others will hold with Hugo that the light
　　Of woman's eyes in far-off heaven was born ;
That till it shone, no starshine lit the night ;
　　That her hand fills with flowers man's wreath of thorn ;

That woman's beauty is the gift supreme,
　　Man's holiest rapture, his divinest bliss ;
That heaven with all its joys was but a dream
　　Till heaven met earth in passion's fiery kiss.

　　　　　　*　　　　　*

Others will dream with Newman that the age
　　Of daily miracles is with us still :
That spirits of good can stem the storm-winds' rage ;
　　That spirits of evil haunt lone lake and hill ;

That Satan stands beside us gazing hard,
　　Eager to tempt, to ruin, to betray ;
That through the June night, fragrant, golden-starred,
　　Winged dark-browed angels wander on their way ;

That still as 'mid far Horeb's desert plains
  Water may gush from strong faith's stricken stone
And God besought by pure hearts send the rains
  Or fruitful sunlight, hearkening from his throne ;

That still ten thousand angels round us stand
  Watchful—and there is blessing in the dream ;
That duty's narrow path, on either hand,
  Is compassed by their bright spears' guardian gleam ;

That still the dead are near,—that still they speak,
  That through the night their ghostly footsteps throng,
That still to-day may humble souls and meek
  Catch here and there one cadence of their song ;

That still o'er every soul some Power bends down,
  Guiding man's foot upon its destined way ;
That every martyred spirit shall wear its crown ;
  That swift help hastens—to the few that pray.

                    *   *

Yet is it not a grander faith than this
  To feel that all things rest beneath the sun ?
What is imagined heaven's most perfect bliss
  To bliss of perfect rest when toil is done ?

Peace endless, peace unbroken and complete,
  Peace that the wings of seraphs may not mar ;
Peace uninvaded by angelic feet ;
  Slumber in lands unseen of sun or star.

Yea, all things rest.   Shall man not rest at all ?
   The sea-wave rests, when stormy days are o'er ;
The woods are restful, when the green leaves fall ;
   The dying sea-weed rests upon the shore.

Death is the goal of life.   Life presses on,
   But ever touches death's lips at the goal.
Not with a deathless light the stars have shone,
   Nor with a deathless light one human soul.

The sun we see that with its fiery gleams
   Traverses heaven shall in the end maybe
Bear life, become the home of human dreams,—
   Bear mountains, shadowy forests, shadeless sea.

The races it shall bear through years of strife
   Shall struggle,—ships shall toss on snowier foam :
Upon the sun, rich in majestic life,
   Shall rise new cities, spire and arch and dome.

A thousand Venices shall lift their towers
   Upon the sun towards skies of ardent air :
Deep groves shall foster unimagined flowers ;
   Love's rapture shall awake—and love's despair.

A thousand Londons there shall stream with life :
   Upon the vast sun's mightier fiery frame
Shall seethe the currents of unmeasured strife,
   Fed by new gods of unknown power and name.

Mars, born again, with eager bound shall leap
   Straight to the fray,—his crimson plume shall wave
Where swords flash thickest and where blood runs deep :
   Huge ships shall founder in their starless grave.

Venus again from bluer waves than ours
   Shall rise, beneath the light of lovelier skies,
Her hair fresh-scented from a thousand flowers,
   With unborn centuries dreaming in her eyes.

She, as she ruled on our poor mortal star,
   Upon the sun shall rule with queenlier sway ;
Make day's bright golden hours diviner far,
   And dark night's hours diviner than the day.

Her shall the unseen amorous hosts aspire
   Beyond all gods to serve, through joy and pain,
For still love's voice shall wake the unknown desire
   And love's sweet sorrow seem man's boundless gain.

Romance, deep-buried when our own star died,
   Shall be reborn within the exalted sun,
Reborn, and loved and crowned and deified,
   New combats fought and kinglier victories won.

But still for ever shall the sense of love
   Old as the skies, in every flower reborn,
Be mightiest power all living hearts to move,
   Ruling the clouds of night, the light of morn.

Yet all shall end !   The life that throbbed along
   The great sun's giant veins shall cease to be :
The lips of Venus silenced in mid-song
   Shall close ; cold stars shall watch a sunless sea.

For even the mighty sun shall surely pass :
   The immense sun-frigate in the vaster main
Of circling air shall plunge its whirling mass
   And cease—its goal of death the sun shall gain.

This being so, shall one frail human soul
   Escape its destiny, and turn and flee,—
Outlive the stars that perish, and control
   The eternal Fate whose touch controls the sea ?

What is a Church, a creed ?   Mere waifs that stray
   Upon the ocean of unmeasured years !
The proudest Church abides but for a day ;
   So long it threatens and thunders in our ears.

Creeds, Churches, Councils, pass—fair is the flower
   The June sun fosters, fair the sunlit foam ;
Yet shall the watchful sun in one brief hour
   Ask, "Where are flowers and foam-bells? Where is Rome?'

TO THE UNIVERSE-GOD.

TO THE UNIVERSE-GOD.

God who leadest human creatures safe through many a path and
    winding way ;
Thou whose word the leaping thunders and the foam-sprent
    warrior-waves obey :

Thou whom not alone the roses worship with their tender-glowing
    bloom
But, besides, the waving grasses gleaming round about the granite
    tomb :

Thou whom all the ancient nations sought, and brought their gifts
    to thine abode ;
Thou through whom the heart of Jesus with the eternal perfect
    pity glowed :

Thou through whom our country's glory reached its splendid
    perfect flower indeed ;
Thou who gavest to the people Love for sign and Freedom for a
    creed :

Still thou livest,—livest surely?   God, thou art not dead, as
some men say,
Men who preach the saws of Science and they win the people to
their way?

Nay, thou livest, livest surely.   Far beyond the fiery whirl of
fate
Thou the God of Love art thronéd, King on whom the giant ages
wait.

Through a thousand mystic voices thou hast spoken to unnumbered years,
Thrilled the heart of priest and singer, thrilled man's fervent soul
to fire or tears.

Thou wast in the old religions, God of glittering war and white-
robed peace ;
Thou wast in the face of Venus, thou didst tread with her the
shores of Greece.

Thou wast in the buoyant waters leaping round her rising from
the wave ;
To her hands their deathless magic thine hand full of stranger
magic gave.

Thou didst give to her for ever power beyond all gods and kings
of time,
Granting her the eternal sweetness that makes honey-sweet the
cup of crime.

For all sins of passion doubtless have in them the sweetness that
    redeems.
Harlot-queen was Theodora ? Yet the world on her strange sweet-
    ness dreams.

Though Elijah's power is broken, though the centuries own no
    more his spell,
Still the light that conquers ages flashes from the eyes of Jezebel.

Is not sweet-lipped fair Delilah passionate still within the realms
    of Art ?
She who lured the love of Samson—still imperial o'er each pain-
    ter's heart.

While on Holyrood the gazer still looks down from rocky heights
    and green
One undying thought must haunt him, still he meets the sweet
    eyes of the queen.

Sin-marred—granted—yet immortal, flower of France and Scot-
    land, Mary waits ;
Her live presence thrills the poet as he steps within her palace-
    gates.

Pass alone through Edinburgh when the Northern starry midnight
    gleams,—
Still the thought is ever of Mary, still her soul pervades the city's
    dreams.

Pass again through Edinburgh when the white streets glitter in
the dawn,—
Still her face is ever present, never from the wanderer's heart
withdraw n. ·

*   *

All the gods of Greece are deathless, Schiller sang their funeral
chant in vain,
For the gods of love shall triumph, victors over all the gods of
pain.

Fruitless was the funeral singing, for the gods in every age reborn
Still with love repay their lovers and their foes with the old
Olympian scorn.

Still their laughter from Olympus, from a thousand star-kissed
peaks beside,
Rings, resounds, and will for ever; still along the clouds their
chariots glide.

Oh, the Immortals ne'er were mortal ! Milton's passionate Hymn
for nought was sung.
Time their thrones defy for ever, Venus' brow was never aught
but young.

Stronger are they than the singer. As we read his mighty Hymn
to-day
Still we feel that those Immortals are more deathless even than
his lay.

Kingsley, Keats, with truer vision sang the old gods still o'er all
  supreme,
Knew that ever star-crowned Venus reimbues with magic first
  love's dream ;

Knew that, though the world may fancy that the war-god never
  more will reign,
Still Mars' heart grows wild with rapture over many a blood-
  soaked battle-plain.

*   *

Thou the eternal cosmic Ruler, thou the vast unalterable Lord,
Art in all of these thy servants, thine hand sways Mars' crimson-
  bladed sword.

In the gods and in the people thou the Spirit of all things hast
  thy part ;
Thou wast in the ancient temples, in the splendours of Athenian
  Art.

All true souls and noble found thee, thee the unchanging God,
  the deathless One,
In the million stars of midnight, in the flowers, the sea-waves and
  the sun.

In strange shrines of many a goddess thou wast hidden, thou
  the God supreme,
Light behind the deadly darkness, truth within the interminable
  dream.

Never one soul quite escaped thee. Thou its Maker hadst a word
　　for each.
Through wild sins and wild contritions thou hadst ceaseless
　　power to raise and teach.

Thou didst thunder over Sinai, thou didst stablish David on his
　　throne ;
Through the starless midnight darkness thou didst speak to
　　Solomon, alone.

Wives who brought him soft-lipped pleasure thou didst for king
　　Solomon provide,—
Many a tender-hearted maiden, many a dark-eyed snowy-breasted
　　bride.

Wast not thou within that heaven, when fast wearying of past star-
　　lit skies
Aging Abraham thy servant found another heaven in Hagar's
　　eyes ?

When her beauty recreated all the sense of godship in his veins,
Made the sun descend in gladness, golden o'er the interminable
　　plains—

Clouded Sarah's heart with anger, but renewed the faith in
　　Abraham's soul
That a God of love was leading, leading on from birth-star to the
　　goal.

Wast not thou within the pleasure winning praise for thee from
    Jacob's tongue
When he, tired of aging Leah, found that Rachel's favouring lips
    were young ?

Wast not thou within the pleasure when Bathsheba to king
    David came,
When, the first sweet time, he kissed her,—when the king's touch
    stirred her heart to flame ?

Was not then the pleasure godlike ? Wast not thou within the
    bridal room,
Lighting with love's flame the darkness, with thy star-fires all the
    outer gloom ?

Dost not thou when lovers mingle, though man's sword-thrust
    waits them with the light,
Hush the stormy winds to silence, fill with joy the imperishable
    night—

Fill the solemn air with sweetness, so that when the one glad hour
    is done
Heart may cry to heart responding, " Surely love's stars have out-
    shone the sun ! "

Hast not thou, thou Power omniscient, watching over stars that
    crowd the skies
Still reserved the light of passion, unrevealed save only in
    woman's eyes ?

Lovelier than the leagues of starlight, purer than the heavens
    where great suns gleam,
Is the light that passion kindles, even as truth is lovelier than the
    dream.

*   *

Thou art deep within all pleasure—thou who scatterest on the
    hills the snows
Art as well within the fragrance of the luscious crimson-petalled
    rose.

Thou who o'er the viewless summits passest like the thunder-
    footed storm
Art as well within the valleys,—grace thou givest to the wood-
    nymph's form.

Thou wast in the soul of Phidias when within the imperishable
    stone
Deep he graved eternal beauty,—and the dream of beauty yet
    unknown.

For in every noble statue sleeps a dream of wonder unrevealed,—
Something that the stars have seen not, something that the sweet
    earth cannot yield.

From the statue's lips of triumph comes a murmur, "Not yet all
    is done !
Lovelier than all earthly beauty waits beyond the moonlight and
    the sun."

Thou, immortal Spirit of beauty, speakest thus through lips of
    flawless stone,
And through other than the statue's, through the model's soft lips'
    living tone.

While the man can mould the statue, thou alone with loving
    touch and warm
Canst enshrine thy dream of beauty in the woman's lovelier
    living form.

Thou the eternal heavens' own Sculptor sendest forth the products
    of thy skill,
Shapes that haunt man's heart for ever, eyes that dazzle and the
    lips that thrill.

        *   *

Through all poets thou hast spoken, leading each along the
    darkling ways ;
Crowning each with thorns of sorrow, then with star-crowns woven
    of deathless rays.

Unto each some word eternal thou dost give—the power to raise
    or smite ;
Music of the golden morning or the dark storm-music of the
    night :

Power to speak thy timeless message on man's planet to the sons
    of time ;
Power to make love's dream immortal, power to make a moment's
    bliss sublime.

                                      Q

Fragrance of a million blossoms on the breezes every morning
    dies,
But the flower within the poem blooms beneath thought's ever-
    radiant skies.

Fragrance of unnumbered passions on the wind of time is wafted
    far,
But a mighty poem's passion, changeless, shares the life of sun or
    star.

Through the Churches thou hast spoken, through the priests of
    heaven and priests of gloom,
Even through fierce Torquemada, rapt apostle of the fiery doom.

Thou didst strew with piteous victims all the floors of hell in
    other years,
Filling all thine heaven with fragrance, all thy night-black hell
    with groans and tears.

Thou didst build thy darkling dungeons, thou didst bid the
    leaping hell-fires flare ;
Thou wast in the heart of Mary, heart that bade brave Cranmer's
    heart despair.

Thou art in the hearts whose passion now proclaims that man is
    free at last ;
Thou art in the fearless present, as thou wast in the subservient
    past.

Thou wast in the heart of Kingsley when that fiery genius-heart
    was young,
When to Kingsley's soul the sea-wind full of mystic power and
    sweetness sung.

Thou didst teach the heart of Kingsley, as he wandered over
    moor and fell,
Secrets of the flowers and sunlight, faith in heaven and disbelief
    in hell.

Thou, the Spirit of all the ages, who hadst spoken through
    Augustine, Paul,
Acrid Knox and bitter Calvin, spakest now through one the
    highest of all—

Highest in this, that through his message rang no trumpet fierce
    with angry doom
But the song of winds of summer, aweless chant of love that
    mocked the tomb.

All the Church was ranked against him—on his side the star-
    shine and the sun,
On his side the chainless sea-waves,—sun and stars and waves
    and Kingsley won.

When he entered life, the hell-fires still within the Church's pale
    flamed high ;
Priests still thundered to the sinner, "Godless wretch, believe
    (in us), or die ! "

When he passed from life, the hell-fires, thanks to Kingsley, all
    were on the wane ;
Love's great fearless tireless warrior had not lived and sung and
    fought in vain.

Paul, Augustine, Calvin, lighted—in those ages that perchance
    was well—
More enduring fame is Kingsley's, that his hand put out the
    fires of hell.

*   *

Hell shall end for woman likewise, lurid hell where ceaseless bale-
    fires gleam ;
She shall rise, superb, immortal, changing into love's wild
    passion's dream.

Though for ages vast, unnumbered, she content has been half
    queen, half slave,
Heedless how or what she squandered, so that only her generous
    instinct gave :

Though for ages she has given, winning not the high return she
    sought,
Yet her sweet deferred pure triumph waits her in the dawning
    age of thought.

Thou who hast watched her tribulation, watched her anguish
    through the darkling years,
Spirit of love not only of passion, thou hast heard her moans
    and marked her tears.

Not one maid in Eastern harem sold and wrecked that man's
    fierce lust might reign
But shall win rich restitution, in some sphere where joy shall
    balance pain.

Not one girl in modern London ruined and soiled for some man's
    passing whim
But shall in the end be queenlike, bring deliverance it may be to
    him.

Thou dost keep divinest record : not one silent sacrifice of tears
But shall see its hope accomplished after it may be twice a
    thousand years.

Time is nought, and thou art deathless—thou on whom thou
    willest canst bestow
Life on life in which to blossom, endless years in which the soul
    may grow.

Flowers on earth for a million ages, these have lit the ways with
    boundless bloom,—
Thou the Spirit of love retainest still thy fairest flowers en-
    wrapped in gloom.

Woman's is the unknown future—man's has been the long past
    dark with crime ;
Now through many a golden era woman's heart shall make man's
    heart sublime.

She shall bring the earth redemption,—fit our star to hold communion high
With bright sister-stars and sinless, glittering spotless in the
untainted sky.

For all stars may hold communion, all the planets' souls are
doubtless one ;
Star to star may speak responsive, moon to white-souled moon,
and sun to sun.

Woman on our earth may doubtless render earth as pure and man
as free
As pure stars and starry races hidden in blue mist on the astral
sea.

Not alone on earth thou toilest : in the countless stars that
traverse night
Thou the Spirit of all art regnant, filling all the cloudy tracts
with light.

Rivers flashing hues of sapphire, emerald groves and opal-coasted
isles,
Waves that welcome ardent sunrise with a thousand golden-
rippling smiles ;

Boundless plains and giant forests, mountains lordlier than our
hearts can dream,
These upon the stars thou rulest—icy wastes on phantom-planets
gleam.

Titan Andes, Himalayas, heights that dazzle with perpetual snows,
Bowers wherein the flowers fade never, deathless lily, never-
    darkening rose :

Bowers wherein pure love speaks ever, love more soft-voiced than
    our planet hears,
Shores where passion's richer rapture thrills far tenderer souls to
    sweeter tears :

These in unknown realms thou swayest, realms where suns are
    scattered like the grains
Flying abroad in windy harvests, torn by tempest from| the
    golden wains.

Lo ! the brain of man turns dizzy at the thought of sky-leagues
    stretching far ;
Never gate nor wall nor barrier—past each outpost still another
    star.

Is there any farthest outpost, any silent sentry-star that waits
Guardian on the dim sky's borders, watchful at the invulnerable
    gates ?

Nay ! beyond, another sentry—still another, ceaseless through the
    night ;
Still another's bright spear glittering, still another helm of fiery
    light.

Human brain may well turn giddy, human thought will never
    reach the goal :
Yet the Ruler of the star-waste hath his temple also in the soul.

Opinions of the Press.

A LOST MOTHER.

Dedicated to the Great Company of Mourners upon Earth with the hope that for one and all of us comfort may be at hand.

One Volume, Fcap. 4to, with Rubricated Initials, antique boards, 4s. 6d.
A Large Paper Edition is also published at 7s. 6d. *net.*

Both Editions contain an excellent Autotype reproduction of Mr. W. BELL SCOTT'S etching of BLAKE'S highly-finished water-colour drawing, illustrating the words "*There shall be no more death, neither sorrow, nor crying, neither shall there be any more pain: for the former things are passed away.*" The original drawing is in the British Museum, and was probably done by Blake as an addition to those published in the series for Blair's *Grave.*

Mr. STOPFORD BROOKE, who read the poem in MS., wrote as follows : "I find your poem a very beautiful thing. It seems to me as true as it is fair, and as sweetly thought as it is well done. It is a poem for all who have lost their earthly love to keep by them and to cherish."

"Mr. George Barlow's new poem, *A Lost Mother,* is a sustained elegy or lament, giving expression at great length to the thoughts, fancies, ideas, questionings, and meditations that come into a poet's mind when it is clouded by a heavy affliction. . . . The work is one of a more sustained effort than Mr. Barlow has yet given to the world. He has produced a poem not only worthy of his reputation, but one likely to confirm and extend it."—*Scotsman.*

"The present poem is inspired by, and dedicated to, the memory of a mother recently lost, to whom the poet seems to have been in a rare degree attached. . . . It is good to meet with speculative thought

I

embodied in clear and straightforward language, as it is throughout the poem ; it is sad to feel, and feel with, the growing depression of thought upon the secret, as much the secret as ever, which underlies and moves the whole of this poem :—

> 'The saddest century since the news went round
> That death was sceptreless and Christ was crowned,'

Mr. Barlow calls this period of ours.   In Tennyson's acceptance of the time as the embodiment of the law of progress, and in some way accordant with the revealed religion which never lost its hold upon the Laureate's mind, Mr. Barlow cannot share.   He is one of the many who rebel against the pitiless miracles of science as removing 'the Lord so far away'; as shedding about the glorious story and meaning of the Resurrection a veil of the dead years which is more than the lapse of time itself would warrant. Happy—happy, indeed—they whose faith can be serenely triumphant over it all, and watch without perplexity and yet with open mind the advance of that Spirit of the Time which weighs to the ground many a heart as earnest and as yearning as Mr. Barlow's would appear to be. . . . The man with the poet's gifts—and there is no doubt there about Mr. Barlow— who feels the odd thing called 'inspiration' and wonders whence it cometh, wants his inspirer.   His earlier verse Mr. Barlow attributes to his mother's constant presence and sympathy. . . . Mr. Barlow is a sad singer ; but he is amongst those who sing."—*Spectator*.

"Ce n'est pas seulement par l'exquise perfection de la forme, l'harmonie du vers, la magique sonorité des syllabes, que se distingue le nouveau volume de notre eminent collaborateur George Barlow.   La douleur y éclate à chaque strophe, une douleur mâle, sans emportements comme sans colère, dans une émotion poignante qui remue et qui etreint.   Le poète y chante sa mère morte, et pour pleurer celle qui le berçait, il se refait petit enfant.   Ce sont les souvenirs de l'enfance première qu'il évoque.   Puis, le lyrisme l'emporte, la poésie, comme le coursier de Mazeppa, le jette sur son dos et l'entraine.

De pareilles oeuvres, du reste, ne s'analysent point.   Il faut les lire et se pénétrer du charme intense qui s'en dégage.   Il faut s'identifier avec la douleur du poète et il est nécessaire pour cela, de l'avoir ressenti.   Si je ne craignais d'offusquer et d'effaroucher l'excessive modestie de George Barlow, je dirais que son poème a réveillé en moi le frisson de douloureuse épouvante que j'avais ressenti en lisant pour la première fois le formidable *Pauca Meae* des *Contemplations*."—M. GEORGES LEFÈVRE, in *La Revue des Revues*.

"There is no sense of exaggeration, though the author carries us with him through all the moods of passion and regret. But he makes us feel with convincing force that he and his mother were united by a tenderness and a sympathy so exceptional that they cannot be measured by conventional standards. . . . With true instinct Mr. Barlow makes his own sorrow serve merely as the foundation of his poem. His thought is centred in his personal loss, but is not confined within that narrow circle. It reaches far out into human experience and touches greater issues. . . . The poem undoubtedly justifies the author's claim to the title of poet : the evidence of genuine power is unmistakable. . . . The volume contains many other passages no less striking and suggestive, but the extracts we have given sufficiently indicate its character and attest its excellence."—*Literary World.*

"Mr. Barlow's position as a poet was assured the moment his work entitled *The Pageant of Life* was published. His second work *From Dawn to Sunset* increased his reputation, and now we have *A Lost Mother*, in which the poet bewails, in manly and touching lines, the death of his mother. . . . There is true poetry on every page, and we welcome Mr. Barlow as a worthy candidate for a niche in the temple of fame.—*Publishers' Circular.*

"Were these lines of lesser quality than they are, criticism and they would needs stand apart. The subject consecrates them. It is a high compliment to Mr. Barlow to compare his poem with *In Memoriam*, but the comparison is one which will naturally strike the reader. . . . What is extremely touching in the poem is the passionate affection that the sight of his mother's physical weakness and frailness drew from him. 'So sweet it is—the weakness of old age.'"—*Bookseller.*

"The poem is, as the title suggests, a threnody in memory of the poet's mother, and is the most restrained, chastened, and dignified piece of work which Mr. Barlow has ever done. That it should be as striking or as original as his very remarkable work, *The Pageant of Life*, could scarcely from the nature of the subject be expected, but it has, on the other hand, a note of sincerity and tenderness which give rare dignity to the poem, and it is marked, moreover, by an entire absence of anything which could startle or offend people of old-fashioned tastes and beliefs. . . . No one who reads even casually any of the mournful but musical verses of *A Lost Mother*, could fail to recognise them as the work of a poet, and a true one. Some of the stanzas towards the close, in which Mr. Barlow contrasts his mother's faith, even in the hour of death, with his own doubts and misgivings, are very beautiful. But, indeed, the poem is a beautiful one throughout, and contains much that must appeal to every reader."—*Sylvia's Journal.*

Crown 8vo. Cloth, 6/-.

FROM DAWN TO SUNSET.

"In his recently published volume, *From Dawn to Sunset*, Mr. George Barlow manifests in quite an equal degree, what he has already shown in his *Pageant of Life*, a power sufficient to place him in the same rank with Tennyson, Swinburne, and Matthew Arnold."—*Westminster Review.*

"*From Dawn to Sunset* ought materially to add to the reputation which Mr. Barlow gained by his *Pageant of Life*. In many of his ethical and philosophical poems he reaches sublimity."—*St. James's Gazette.*

"The many admirers of *The Pageant of Life* will welcome its author's latest work, which is destined, we believe, to occupy a permanent and honoured place in the poetical literature of the Victorian era. Mr. George Barlow is not only a poet, he is also a profound thinker ; for which reason alone his works would deserve more than an evanescent fame. We cannot, in the space at our command, do justice to this remarkable volume. Although some of Mr. Barlow's ideas may startle people by their boldness, yet they cannot fail to command admiration by reason of their fearless sincerity even from those who are unable to agree with the theories propounded. Happily there are many parts that will evoke no controversial feeling or arouse anything but admiration. Amongst these must be mentioned the sonnets and lyrics interspersed throughout the volume, many of which are gems of the first water. *From Dawn to Sunset* is emphatically a book to be read."—*Vanity Fair.*

"Mr. Barlow has a genuine gift of song. In the great variety of poems in this volume he sings in many keys, and his voice is always flexible and melodious."—*Scotsman.*

"*The Pageant of Life* will be remembered for the powerful impression which its bold thought and fine diction made on the public mind. Readers will be charmed with much of the poetry Mr. Barlow now offers. . . . Many of the poems undoubtedly will survive the fate of verse that is verse and nothing more."—*Manchester Examiner.*

"Mr. Barlow's power of producing fluent and readable verse is remarkable."—*Academy.*

"*From Dawn to Sunset* is an important book. As a singer Mr. Barlow can lay claim to a rank which few would question. He stands forward as an inspired teacher of mankind. . . . His poetry must be admitted to overflow with passion, eloquence, and music."—*Black and White.*

" Mr. Barlow is unquestionably a singer of courage and skill."—*Glasgow Herald*.

" The author is a man of many moods, intensely affected by the problems of modern life, yet refusing to sink into pessimism or to retire into mysticism."—*Light*.

" *From Dawn to Sunset* contains many lyrical gems. The book is replete with passages of the highest poetry . . . it has been a real treat to us to peruse it."—*Anglo-American*.

" *The Pageant of Life* proved that Mr. Barlow is a true poet, and if further proof were needed it would be furnished by the present work. There are many passages of exquisite sweetness and great force, passages that remain in the memory and keep the soul aflame long after the book has been laid aside. Only poetry of a high order can do this, nor is it too much to say that Mr. Barlow is one of the truest and most stimulating singers of his day. . . . *From Dawn to Sunset* is a book that should be read by all students of humanity and all lovers of true poetry."—*Publishers' Circular*.

" Mr. Barlow has shown us again and again that he can write lyrics and verses which are not only musical and appeal directly to the ear, but have poetry and feeling, as *A Year Ago* and other pieces in this volume will amply prove."—*Daily Graphic*.

" Mr. George Barlow has just collected his works into one volume under the title *From Dawn to Sunset*. The first book contains *The Song of Youth*, the second *The Song of Manhood*, and the third *The Song of Riper Manhood*. The reader will thus be able to trace the various stages of the poet's growth. If his earlier style is fresh and buoyant, his later is stronger and more thoughtful. As should always be the case, the tree in autumn bears the riper fruit."—*Daily Chronicle*.

" Mr. Barlow's *Pageant of Life* showed real power, and great things were anticipated from its author. There are some noble passages in the present volume. The lines to ' the green old slopes of Harrow Hill ' will ring pleasantly in the ears of many an old Harrovian."—*Morning Post*.

" Mr. Barlow writes fluently, and with touches of really noble verbal music."—*Birmingham Daily Post*.

" *From Dawn to Sunset* is a volume of poetry which may be perused with unfeigned pleasure. The range of subjects is unusually exhaustive, and the reader may find something to suit his taste in almost any mood."—*Liverpool Daily Post*.

" Mr. Barlow's verses are marked by genuine feeling, graceful diction, and a skilful use of many verse forms. We are likely to hear more of him."—*Yorkshire Post*.

5

Second Edition, Crown 8vo. Cloth, 4/6.

THE PAGEANT OF LIFE.

𝔄n 𝔈pic of 𝔐an. 𝔍n 𝔉ibe 𝔅ooks.

" A new poet has arisen among us ; an indisputable poet, orcible, graceful, earnest, courageous ; having something of real interest and great moment to say, and knowing how to express his strong, bold thoughts in words of extraordinary power, and lines of rare beauty. . . . Mr. Barlow is manifestly a sincere deist, worshipping the Supreme Being with fervent intensity and profound conviction. Those who do not share his opinions, and may deprecate the tremendous frankness with which he propounds them, cannot fail to be impressed by the passionate reality of his reverence for the omnipotent, omniscient, and omnipresent Creator, to whom some of the finest of his magnificent invocations are addressed. . . . In Book II.—entitled *A Masque of Human Life*—of this remarkable poem, Mr. Barlow makes men, women, and children disclose their joys and sorrows, views and idiosyncrasies. There is an episode of extraordinary force, setting forth the passion of a high-minded worldling for a poor chorus-girl. It is in Books III. and IV. that Mr. Barlow's lyrical *chefs d'œuvre* must be looked for. There musicians will find good store of exquisite verses, such as should inspire them with melodies of surpassing beauty. Here, for instance, is one verse of a Spring Song, worthy to have been set by Mendelssohn himself. . . . We are unable, to our regret, to devote any further space to Mr. Barlow's Epic or to its incidental lyrics. His fellow-countrymen should read the poem ; many must condemn its audacious outspokenness ; few will withhold admiration from its lofty thoughts and splendid diction, which entitle its author to high rank among the ' British Bards ' of the Victorian age."—*Daily Telegraph.*

" Very many of the single lyrics are full of beauty, and rich in music. That Mr. Barlow is a genuine and often a very sweet singer, it were vain to deny."—*Manchester Examiner.*

" This is a very remarkable book : nor is it with any intention to depreciate the value of the verse contained therein, if we say that the preface is by no means its least striking portion. Twenty years ago such a preface, so calm, so clear, so modest in intention, and yet so entirely heretical in its assertions, would have been impossible."—*Universal Review.*

"Rare gifts of mind and song. Since Byron, never has 'British Philistinism' been scouted in such bitter terms as by Mr. Barlow's 'Satan.' . . . Of undoubted power and quite exceptional poetical merit."—*Morning Post*.

"Has made its mark, and is bound to create a deep and lasting impression. Much of the poetry is very fine. Some of it rises to audacious heights rarely aspired to by human genius. The book will arouse the inquiry of all. Mr. Barlow is not only a true poet, he is also a great thinker."—*Birmingham Mail*.

"Many of the lyrics and ballads are particularly bright and good."—*Academy*.

"This is a work by a new poet—a great poet—a disciple of Shelley, it would seem, and to be, if he likes, as great as his master. *The Song of Christ* is perhaps the noblest of all the noble songs, ballads, and odes in this wonderful book. . . . The poem, as a poem, may stand beside *Paradise Lost* and Byron's *Cain*—more human than the first, more tender than the second."—*Metropolitan*.

"Mr. Barlow is a master of passionate and picturesque verse. His command of imagery, the force and fire of his ideas, the clearness and vigour of his style, are unmistakable. There are many powerful and beautiful passages in this book, and hardly a weak line from cover to cover. . . . Mr. Barlow's thoughts on women and children are always good and true."—*Light*.

"That wonderful book, *The Pageant of Life*, which has created so great a sensation in the literary world."—*Vanity Fair*.

"This extraordinary Epic poem in five books, which treats of life and love and sin and misery, and in which 'Christ' and 'Satan' figure as rival combatants."—*Spectator*.

"We have enjoyed reading Mr. Barlow's book. It is daring and interesting. . . . There is no part of Mr. Barlow's book which lacks interest. He seems to have speculated much, and felt keenly. His sympathies are true and his dreams have wings. He has many of the gifts for which we love poets; originality, tenderness, grace, beauty of thought and expression. We hope our readers may spend as pleasant hours over his pages as did we."—*To-day*.

7

London
SWAN SONNENSCHEIN & CO.

⩀ Trieste

Trieste Publishing has a massive catalogue of classic book titles. Our aim is to provide readers with the highest quality reproductions of fiction and non-fiction literature that has stood the test of time. The many thousands of books in our collection have been sourced from libraries and private collections around the world.

The titles that Trieste Publishing has chosen to be part of the collection have been scanned to simulate the original. Our readers see the books the same way that their first readers did decades or a hundred or more years ago. Books from that period are often spoiled by imperfections that did not exist in the original. Imperfections could be in the form of blurred text, photographs, or missing pages. It is highly unlikely that this would occur with one of our books. Our extensive quality control ensures that the readers of Trieste Publishings books will be delighted with their purchase. Our staff has thoroughly reviewed every page of all the books in the collection, repairing, or if necessary, rejecting titles that are not of the highest quality. This process ensures that the reader of one of Trieste Publishings titles receives a volume that faithfully reproduces the original, and to the maximum degree possible, gives them the experience of owning the original work.

We pride ourselves on not only creating a pathway to an extensive reservoir of books of the finest quality, but also providing value to every one of our readers. Generally, Trieste books are purchased singly - on demand, however they may also be purchased in bulk. Readers interested in bulk purchases are invited to contact us directly to enquire about our tailored bulk rates. Email: customerservice@triestepublishing.com

You May Also Like

Woman in the Pulpit

Frances E. Willard

ISBN: 9781760571832
Paperback: 184 pages
Dimensions: 6.14 x 0.39 x 9.21 inches
Language: eng

The Logic of Will: A Study in Analogy

Helen Wodehouse

ISBN: 9781760579579
Paperback: 192 pages
Dimensions: 6.14 x 0.41 x 9.21 inches
Language: eng

You May Also Like

Reminiscences of an Indianian: From the Sassafras Log behind the Barn in Posey County to Broader Fields

J. A. Lemcke

ISBN: 9781760571467
Paperback: 242 pages
Dimensions: 6.14 x 0.51 x 9.21 inches
Language: eng

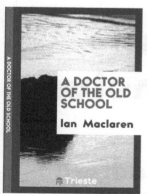

A Doctor of the Old School

Ian Maclaren

ISBN: 9781760574567
Paperback: 224 pages
Dimensions: 6.14 x 0.47 x 9.21 inches
Language: eng

www.triestepublishing.com

You May Also Like

Shut Your Mouth and Save Your Life

George Catlin

ISBN: 9781760570491
Paperback: 118 pages
Dimensions: 6.14 x 0.25 x 9.21 inches
Language: eng

The Epistle to Diognetus

L. B. Radford

ISBN: 9781760570934
Paperback: 106 pages
Dimensions: 6.14 x 0.22 x 9.21 inches
Language: eng

www.triestepublishing.com

You May Also Like

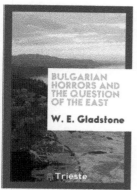

Bulgarian horrors and the question of the East

W. E. Gladstone

ISBN: 9781760571146
Paperback: 46 pages
Dimensions: 6.14 x 0.09 x 9.21 inches
Language: eng

Snow-bound: A Winter Idyl

John Greenleaf Whittier

ISBN: 9781760571528
Paperback: 64 pages
Dimensions: 5.5 x 0.13 x 8.25 inches
Language: eng

Find more of our titles on our website. We have a selection of thousands of titles that will interest you. Please visit

www.triestepublishing.com

Printed in Australia
AUHW011204041120
336647AU00011B/28